BEYOND HATE
A SCREEN PLAY
Author: Tiêu Dao Bảo Cự
Layout: Nguyễn Thành
Cover: Lê Hân & Nguyễn Thành
Painting for cover: Khánh Trường
Nhân Ảnh Publisher 2020
ISBN: 978-1989705766
Copyright © 2020 byTieuDaoBaoCu

TIÊU DAO BẢO CỰ

BEYOND HATE

A SCREEN PLAY

NHÂN ẢNH
2020

The book you now hold in your hand is the English translation of a screenplay I created from a short story that I wrote and published several years ago. This book could not have been possible without the help of many friends who contributed as translators and editors over a period of two years. To them I own an eternal debt of gratitude, the more so when they all wish to remain anonymous. Please enjoy the book, and be mindful that any and all errors that you may find are mine and mine alone.

Tiêu Dao Bảo Cự.

THEMES

This is a story about some of the sufferings after America's involvement in the Vietnam War ended (1954-1975).

The story begins with the rape of a 16-year-old Vietnamese girl by a black Amerasian. The rape raises numerous issues and questions. Can people still hate long after the war has ended? How should an intellectual live and think when life reaches a dead end? Can love and trust overcome hatred, envy, and separation? When one's life is full of hatred and lies, can happiness be achieved by losing one's mind?

THE CHARACTERS

The characters have no specific name. They are generic.

THE MAN – Around 40 to 50 years old. Skinny with sunken cheeks. Former high school literature teacher prior to 1975. After the North's victory over the South, was allowed to keep his job, but was then fired for harboring anti-government thoughts. Tried hard to make a living by working at various odd jobs. Settled for selling used books on the sidewalk. Tormented and utterly unhappy for having to live in poverty and destitution in a society that has no use for his knowledge and experience. Extremely confused, angry, and desiring only revenge upon learning that his daughter was raped by a black Amerasian. Relented when the love between his daughter and the black Amerasian became apparent to him. Became despondent and listless when the black Amerasian didn't return from America after 5 years as promised. Depressed and emaciated, has started having strange dreams.

THE GIRL'S MOTHER – Wife of the Man. Around 40 to 50 years old. Used to be a vegetable grower. Became a housewife and peddler of sundry goods after her marriage. Raised in the traditional way with minimal education. Suffered greatly upon learning that her daughter was raped by an Amerasian. Afraid that people would make fun of her family if her daughter and the Amerasian got married.

THE GIRL - Around 16 years old. Dropped out of high school to help her family in dire financial conditions. Very pretty. Well read for her age since her father used to teach literature and still has a sizable collection of books. Was initially disoriented by the rape, but later turned around because she knew him before the rape and was somewhat attracted to him. Met with him secretly a few more times after the rape and accepted his love for her. Spent a night with him in a cave. Believed that he would marry her when he got back from America. Waited 5 years for his return. Became despondent and suffered a nervous breakdown.

THE AMERASIAN – Around 20 years old. Amerasian. Tall with light black skin. Curly hair. Quite handsome. Grew up rejected and despised in a society that once considered Americans as enemies. Met the girl, a neighbor, by chance. Fell in love with her after a few encounters. Lost control and raped her. Was profoundly remorseful. Asked the girl and his mother for forgiveness. Promised that once repatriated to the USA as an Amerasian, would return within 5 years to marry the girl. Discovered, targeted and hunted down by a policeman for criminal prosecution while gathering the paperwork needed to leave the country. Was able to convince the policeman to let him off by showing him how sincere and deep his love for the girl was after a deadly chase. Promised the girl under pain of death that he would return within 5 years. Did not return for reasons unknown.

THE AMERASIAN'S MOTHER–Around 40 to 50 years old. Husband died of drunkenness. Got involved with a black American GI while working at a US military base. Lived with the GI a short time. Got pregnant just as the GI was being transferred. Lost contact with him. Gave birth to the Amerasian. Raised him until he was a young man. Accepted all the name-calling that came with having an Amera-sian son. Started to collect the needed paperwork to apply for her son to emigrate to the US when the US government began allowing Amerasians to do so. Suffered greatly when the rape took place. Spent a lot of money and effort trying to save her son. Bribed one policeman to help her son escape prosecution. Convinced another policeman to hunt down and prosecute her son in order to punish him. Was able to emigrate to the US with her son. Left behind a legacy of immense pain and suffering to the family of the girl her son had raped.

THE AMERICAN SOLDIER – around 30 to 40 years old. Black, tall, with a gentle-looking face. Posted to a base on the outskirts of a village. Fell in love with a local woman (the Amerasian's mother) who worked there. Lived with her and truly loved her. Had wanted to marry her, but the war caused them to lose track of one other. Left behind a child whom he may or may not not have even known about.

POLICEMAN A – Around 30 to 40 years old. Tall and stocky. With a large face and piggish eyes. Typical physique of a corrupt cop. Took advantage of the rape to extort gold from the Amerasian's mother. Had to deal with Police-man B, who hated and wanted to hunt down the Amerasian to punish him. Protected the Amerasian and his mother, who, eventually, were able to emigrate to America.

POLICEMAN B – Around 30 to 40 years old. Ice-cold expression. Entire family killed along with around 500 others during the My-Lai/Son My massacre in 1968 that shook America. Heard about the rape perpetrated by the Amerasian. Decided to hunt him down, bring him to justice, and punish him even though it was not his case. After several near misses, finally cornered the Amerasian after a dead-ly chase. Listened to the Amerasian, and understood his deep and true love for the girl. Decided to let him go. Felt relieved and at peace with himself.

THE BOY – Around 5 years old. The son of the Amerasian and the girl. He exists only in the dreams of the girl's father.

SUMMARY

One afternoon, when returning home from work and walking past a cemetery, the man hears moaning sounds coming from among the graves. He rushes in to take a look and is shocked to find his own daughter lying on the ground next to a tomb and crying. Her clothes are torn, and there are signs of blood. He understands immediately that his daughter has been raped. He races back out onto the road to look for the perpetrator and sees a tall silhouette running away and disappearing beyond the horizon.

He carries his daughter back to their house at the edge of the cemetery, and he and his wife care for her and ask about what happened. But she says nothing. The old couple are very sad and distraught. They cannot cope with the disaster that has happened to their 15-year-old daughter. After several days of questioning, the old couple guesses that the man who raped their daughter is an Amerasian, who lives in a nearby hamlet and whom they also met previously. The realization that the Amerasian has done this horri ies them.

After thinking it over, the man decides to go to the Amerasian's home to negotiate a way out because he doesn't want the rape story to become public and damage his daughter's as well as the family's reputation. The Amerasian's family consists of only two people: the Amerasian and his mother. The Amerasian is the result of the love between his mother and an American serviceman, who was stationed near the hamlet and who disappeared after the war ended. However, the US government is now implementing a policy whereby Amerasians and their immediate family can immigrate to the US. This presents an oppor-tunity for the Amerasian and his mother to escape their current poverty. When the man tells the mother about the rape, she becomes enraged because she thinks that he wants to extort money from her.

When the Amerasian returns home, his mother questions him about the rape, and he admits that the story she has heard is true. He adds that he knows and loves the girl, is very remorseful, and wants to confess his crime to the girl's parents to seek their forgiveness and find a way to resolve the situation. His confession shocks his mother since his actions could jeopardize their dream of going to America. In the meantime, the father of the girl becomes enraged. He finds an old hunting knife, sharpens it, and decides to use it to get revenge by killing the Amerasian. He hides near the turn off on the road to the Amerasian's house and when he walks by, jumps out to stab him. However, the Amerasian is quick and escapes with only a few scrapes. The Amerasian recognizes his attacker, kneels, asks for forgiveness, confesses his love for the daughter and states his desire for a satisfactory resolution of the affair. The man is surprised by this turn of events and says he accepts for the time being what the Amerasian has said. However, the man demands that the Amerasian and his mother come to his home to discuss the matter.

The supposedly secret story of an Amerasian being

involved in a rape somehow leaks out. Two local policemen become concerned with the story. Policeman A, who is re-sponsible for the area where the Amerasian and his mother live, wants to extort money from them. Policeman B wants to capture and punish the Amerasian because he has a personal grudge to settle with the Americans and anything related to America. During the war, his entire family per-ished during the My Lai/Son My Massacre in 1968.

The Amerasian finds himself in a tense situation. He cannot come to the girl's home to discuss the matter and ask for forgiveness because he must now flee. However, he manages to meet the girl in secret. They talk and come to an understanding, and the girl accepts the Amerasian's love for her and forgives him.

Policeman B contacts the old man and the girl, but cannot prove anything because they do not cooperate with him. He tries to ambush the Amerasian near the girl's house, but cannot capture him. Instead, he sees the Amerasian and the girl behaving like two people in love. One day he catches up with the Amerasian at his house, but cannot arrest him because Policeman A is there and prevents the arrest from taking place. Policeman A continues to threat-en and extort gold from the Amerasian's mother.

Meanwhile, misfortune continues to pile up for the parents of the girl. The roadside shop they own is raided, and ev-erything is confiscated and taken to the Tax Office in a campaign to clean up the street. The father only manages to salvage one book about the Kieu story during the raid. Despondent, he takes the book and wanders all day on the street like a ghost. In the afternoon, he stops by a roadside pub, orders a liter of wine, and drinks until he becomes drunk. It so happens that Policeman A is also in the pub. He goes over to the old man's table to strike up a conversation and to find out more about the old man's daughter and the Amerasian.

Upon receiving news that the Amerasian is hiding in a nearby hamlet, Policeman B sets out to find him. A deadly chase takes place between him and the Amerasian on a hillside tea plantation. The Amerasian is young, strong, and fast, and he continues to put distance between himself and the policeman. Then Policeman B fires his gun and startles the Amerasian. He stumbles, and the policeman catches up with him. The two then argue about the rape the Amerasian allegedly committed. The Amerasian affirms that he loves the girl, and she loves him, and that he will marry her once he gets back from his trip to the U.S. Policeman B feels in his heart the true love the Amerasian has for the girl. When the Amerasian tries to run away, Policeman B raises his gun, and aims at the Amerasian, but, at the last moment before pulling the trigger, he jerks the gun barrel up and shoots at the sky. Policeman B has failed to capture the Amerasian once again, but this time he feels relieved and not bitter as before.

The Amerasian asks the girl for a last meeting on the grassy hill before he leaves for America. On the afternoon of the meeting, high winds and a storm batter the grassy hill. As the girl stumbles and falls in the rain and wind, the Amerasian comes and takes her inside a grotto on the mountain side. They spend the night together, give themselves completely to each other, and find happiness and peace despite their cursed love.

The story ends with a surprise twist. Five years later, the Amerasian returns to marry the girl, who is now a beautiful young woman with a 5-year-old son. The simple wedding takes place at an old house behind the cemetery. Attending the wedding at the invitation of the Amerasian are the two policemen who were involved in his case. Halfway through the wedding, the newlyweds take their young son to revisit the old grotto where the boy was conceived, and from which emerged the now happy life that they have. However, this scene is actually just a dream that plays and replays endlessly inside the mind of the girl's father. In reality, because the Amerasian never returned, the old man has become utterly depressed and lost his mind while the girl looks old and haggard.

The old man wonders, who suffers more, him or his daughter. Could it be that when life is full of lies and hate, losing one's mind can make one happier? But then suddenly one afternoon as the sun is setting, and they are sitting and brooding, the Amerasian returns and looks exactly as the old man has envisioned him in his dreams. No one knows if this is a dream or reality. Or is reality also a dream in the end?

1. THE CEMETERY – OUTSIDE – AFTERNOON

Late afternoon. The golden afternoon sunlight plays on the crosses of the tombs.

An emaciated man walks along the winding path that crosses the cemetery with his head down.

Large, imposing tombs can be seen among lesser and simpler ones. Some of the latter are just shapeless and crum-bling mounds of sand.

Burning incense sticks add an air of dark horror to the cemetery.

> **THE MAN**
>
> (mumbling)
>
> To each his own fate? As for me, I must have been born under an unlucky star.

2. THE CLASSROOM – INSIDE – MORNING (FLASH-BACK)

THE MAN is wearing a white shirt, black pants, and shiny shoes. He is a literature instructor standing on the teacher's platform of a classroom. The students are listening at-tentively to him. On the blackboard is written: "The Story of Kiều". Chalked on the blackboard are the following verses: *"If your fate is to be adrift, resign yourself to it / if your fate is to be noble, accept it"*

> THE MAN
>
> Is it a man's fate or is it true that man is but a victim of society, of a political system?
>
> What do you think?

3. A CITY CORNER – OUTSIDE - MORNING (FLASHBACK)

A man wearing shabby clothes is selling used books on the sidewalk. He is sitting on a little plastic stool. Before him is a plastic sheet with dozens of used books. A passerby stops to pick up a book to inspect it.

> THE MAN
>
> Please look carefully. All books are valuable.
>
> Nowadays you have to come here on the street to find them because the bookstores don't carry them anymore.

4. THE CEMETERY – OUTSIDE – AFTERNOON

Suddenly the man hears sobbing sounds coming from behind a large tomb that is not too far from the road. He steps toward the tomb to get a closer look.

He sees a girl lying crumpled on the ground. Her clothes are torn. On her white skin there are scratch marks and below there is smeared blood. The girl pulls her knees together and cries haltingly.

He lifts the girl up and asks as if shell-shocked.

> **THE MAN**
>
> What happened, my daughter?
>
> Who did this to you?

The girl grasps her father tightly and continues to sob without answering his question. He suddenly understands everything.

> **THE MAN**
>
> Who did this? Who did this? I will kill you!

5. THE CEMETERY – OUTSIDE – AFTERNOON

The man lets go of his daughter and dashes toward the road like a madman. In the darkness, he stumbles and falls several times.

Suddenly he notices a tall, wavering silhouette against, and then disappearing into, the darkening sky.

He stumbles on a mound and falls to the ground. In desperation he bursts into tears.

6. THE GIRL'S HOME – INSIDE – EVENING

The man rises with difficulty and then slowly makes his way back to the tomb to carry his daughter home. The girl is limp in his arms, her hair flopping with each unsteady step her suffering father takes.

7. THE GIRL'S HOME – INSIDE – EVENING

The wooden house has a tin roof and is poor and dilapidated. An oil lamp gives out a weak and flickering light. The front room looks empty as it contains only a flimsy set of living room furniture. The back room is divided into two areas by a curtain.

Brought home by her father, bathed and cleaned up by her mother, who has also changed her clothes and put ointments on her wounds, the girl is recovering, but she refuses to say anything.

> **THE GIRL'S MOTHER**
>
> (Sobbing as she talks to her husband)
>
> Father, what happened to our daughter?
>
> **THE MAN**
>
> She has been…She has been…
>
> **THE GIRL'S MOTHER**
>
> What happened to her? Tell me? Who did this?

(In his mind's eye, THE MAN sees the silhouette of the tall, lanky man against the sky)

> **THE MAN**
>
> It's possible he could be… He could be… But I am not sure.

BEYOND HATE

8. THE GIRL'S HOME – INSIDE – EVENING (FLASHBACK)

THE GIRL'S MOTHER walks to the back of the house. THE MAN is sitting still with his head bent near his daughter's bed.

He remembers how she used to run out to greet him every day when he got back home, how he would kiss her on the cheek, how she would get him a glass of water, and how she would pour water in a basin for him to wash his face.

He remembers the dreams he used to have of her growing up, pretty as a flower, and walking into a university auditorium under the admiring gaze of the male students.

9. THE GIRL'S HOME – INSIDE – EVENING

THE GIRL wakes up, opens her eyes, and looks at her father. THE MAN strokes her hair and gently talks to her.

> THE MAN
>
> Tell your father what happened. Don't be afraid. Was it the Amerasian?

THE GIRL opens her eyes wide. She looks surprised. She neither acknowledges what he has said nor denies it. He understands that he has guessed right. His face suddenly contorts, and he slumps down in his seat.

10. THE CEMETERY – OUTSIDE – EVENING

The man sits by his daughter's bed as she lies there. Dark and painful thoughts fill his mind. Meanwhile, the Amerasian wanders around the cemetery and secretly observes the girl's house. Several times throughout the night, he qui-etly approaches her house and then retreats back to the large tomb where he had his conversation with the girl in the afternoon.

11. A HAMLET ROAD – OUTSIDE – MORNING (FLASH-BACK)

The Amerasian remembers how,when he was a little boy playing with other kids, they used to call him a "bastard" and "Amerasian" even though he was bigger, taller, and stronger than any of them.

He remembers how he cried and ran toward his mother to tell her what the other kids had said. All she could do was to hug him tightly and cry silently.

12. THE GIRL'S HOME – INSIDE – EVENING (FLASH-BACK)

The Amerasian remembers how he met the girl for the first time, when he saw her carrying a heavy load of sticks or a large pail of water and offered to carry it for her. After a while, they became friends and were seen talking to each other.

13. THE CEMETERY – OUTSIDE - EVENING (FLASH-BACK)

In the afternoon, the Amerasian invites the girl to go with him to a big tomb in the cemetery to talk. She happily follows him. They sit and talk with their backs against the tomb, which has a large and shady roof.

Watching the innocent girl plucking and releasing into the wind the yellow petals of a small flower, he feels an ache in his heart. He speaks to her.

THE AMERASIAN

I am going away.

THE GIRL (looking at him with wide-open eyes)

Where?

THE AMERASIAN

Very far away.

THE GIRL

How many kilometers is very far away?

THE AMERASIAN

Thousands and thousands of kilometers away.

THE GIRL

Where is this so faraway place?

He feels that she is very naïve. He wants to hear her

express sadness when he tells her he is going away. But it seems that she does not feel that way. He gives her more details.

> THE AMERASIAN
>
> I am going to America. I have been sponsored to come there as an Amerasian.

This is the first time he refers to himself as an "Amerasian", and this makes him uneasy. He is afraid she might not like it. But she appears unfazed. She looks at him.

> THE GIRL
>
> Yeah, I see. You are an Amerasian. So now Amerasians can go to America?

> THE AMERASIAN
>
> Yes. The paperwork is being processed. I will be leaving next month.

Both remain silent for a moment. He hears his voice reverberate and spread out like the deep and sad sound of a bell over the cemetery now bathed in the yellowish twilight. He suddenly takes the girl's hand and asks, as if in a daze:

> THE AMERASIAN
>
> Will you be sad if I leave? Will you miss me?

The girl doesn't reply, but she doesn't pull her hand back either. She feels the young man's strong, warm hand squeezing hers.

He caresses her hand then bends down to whisper.

THE AMERASIAN

I will go away for a few years, and then I will come back to marry you.

Do you understand what I just said? By then you will be an adult.

Here, the only person close to me is my mother.

He speaks forcefully, decisively -- as if he has long prepared to say these things. The girl still says nothing and keeps her head down.

He starts to caress and then kiss her cheek and neck. The girl resists weakly and as her skin crawls and her mind is filled with pleasure and shame.

His caresses cause her to lose control. He pushes her down and kisses her lips while his hands hurriedly grope her budding breasts as she lies under his muscular body.

The girl becomes scared. She pushes him away and starts to scream. Startled, he presses his hand over her mouth and speaks as he breathes heavily.

THE AMERASIAN

Don't... don't be afraid.

Don't be afraid... I love you

And then the animal instincts of the male take over. He does everything brutally until she passes out.

He now feels fear and remorse. He holds the girl close to him and gently shakes her to bring her back to conscious-ness. She then starts crying softly.

He doesn't know what to do, but then hears a man's footsteps approaching. Silently he slinks away like a cat van-ishing in the half darkness.

14. THE GIRL'S HOME – INSIDE – EVENING

The man and his wife cannot sleep for most of the night. He suffers silently, but his wife screams, curses and cries. They feel completely powerless to deal with the situation as they look at their daughter lying motionless and half asleep on her bed under the yellowish and flickering light of the oil lamp.

Outside of the thatch roof and dilapidated home, the wind suddenly howls over the treetops. Now and then, like the stabs of a sharp knife, the icy and sharp hoots of an owl pierce the frightening darkness that envelops the cemetery.

15. THE GIRL'S HOME – OUTSIDE – MORNING

In the morning, the man asks his wife to walk out into the garden so that they can talk without being overheard by their daughter.

>THE MAN
>
>I already asked her.

While she doesn't acknowledge it, I am almost sure that the perpetrator is the Amerasian who lives in the next hamlet.

THE GIRL'S MOTHER

(startled, as if about to faint, she mumbles)

What? What? Is it the Amerasian? The blackman?

THE MAN

The difficult thing is we didn't catch him in the act, and our daughter refuses to say anything.

I hope that she will return to normal soon and will tell everyone.

But this is a shameful thing.

Should we tell the police?
If we tell the police, we might as well tell everybody in the town, and then how will you and our daughter look everyone in the eyes?

Furthermore, to have proof, our daughter must undergo an examination…

THE GIRL'S MOTHER

(recoiling)

Don't, don't do that! My poor daughter, she has suf-fered enough. Don't torture her more.

The man's face, after the sleepless night, looks ragged and shrunken-- the more so when one notices the deep wrinkle on his forehead, the hollow cheeks, and unshaven stubble. He sits thinking silently and then speaks haltingly.

> **THE MAN**
>
> But we cannot be silent and accept our loss for the rest of our lives because that would be unfair to our daughter. Or, or perhaps we should go talk to him, maybe force him to marry her? What do you think? Would that work?
>
> **THE GIRL'S MOTHER**
>
> (confused and recoiling again)
>
> Marry? This black American? A black Amerasian? She is only 16! How can this be?

The more they talk, the deeper the impasse they find themselves in, and the more their hatred grows. Suddenly the man becomes very angry. He starts screaming.

> **THE MAN**
>
> Or I could go kill him. To avenge our daughter, to make him pay dearly for his crime. The miserable mixed race boy!
>
> **THE GIRL'S MOTHER**
>
> No! That is impossible. You will go to jail if you kill him. And anyway, how could you kill him?
>
> You are weak, while he is like an elephant -- much bigger and much stronger than you.

THE MAN

(His jaws tightening, his eyes glaring)

Why not?

If I can't kill him with my bare hands, I can use a knife or a grenade.

I have ways to kill him.

I will be able to kill him. Do you understand?

16. THE CEMETERY – OUTSIDE – AFTERNOON

Dejected, the man walks away, and his steps take him back to the tomb where his daughter was harmed. He sits down and is surprised that no trace is left of the crime.

He asks himself: "Why was she raped here? Could it be that he abducted her from our house? Is it possible she had sex before with the Amerasian? Could this be possible? Our daughter is very young and naïve, could it be that she had changed, and I hadn't realized? I must go see the Amerasian to talk this out before taking the next step."

17. THE BLACK AMERASIAN'S HOME – OUTSIDE – AFTERNOON

Upon leaving the tomb, the man starts looking for the black Amerasian. He does not have to look far. Many in the nearby neighborhood know where he lives.

The Amerasian's home is at the end of the hamlet. It is a semi-dilapidated house with tin walls and not much better than the man's own. In front of the house is a small courtyard shielded by a hibiscus hedge. He knocks, and a woman, who looks sick, opens the door. He asks immediately:

THE MAN

Excuse me, is this the home of the black Amerasian?

THE AMERASIAN'S MOTHER

Yes.

THE MAN

Is he home?

THE AMERASIAN'S MOTHER

He isn't back from work yet. Is there something you want? I am his mother.

The man stands for a moment as if deciding what to do next and then says.

THE MAN

May I come in to speak with you please?

THE AMERASIAN'S MOTHER

Yes, please come in.

18. THE BLACK AMERASIAN'S HOME – INSIDE – AFTERNOON

The Amerasian's mother invites the man into the living room where there is a used set of furniture. She politely offers him some water in a dirty and yellowish glass.

The man hesitates a bit because he does not know how to start the conversation. In the end, he decides to begin with a cautious, probing question.

> THE MAN
>
> Did your son come home last night and talk to you about anything?

The question surprises the mother.

> THE AMERASIAN'S MOTHER
>
> He was out all night and stayed at a friend's home. He didn't come back until morning.
>
> He didn't talk about anything special.

The man hesitates for a moment as if trying to find a way to talk around the issue about which he has come. But then the feelings burning up inside him make him overcome his caution.

> THE MAN
>
> This may seem intrusive, but may I ask you a question:
>
> What would you think if your son had committed the crime of rape?

The woman opens her eyes wide in horror to stare at the man in front of her. She reacts immediately.

THE AMERASIAN'S MOTHER

No. Never. My son is a good boy. He would never do that...

Who are you to defame my son? What do you want?

THE MAN

Please stay calm, madam. I understand your state of mind.

But please listen to me. I live in the nearby neighborhood.

My house is at the end of the hamlet near the cemetery.

Last night, your son raped my daughter, a girl who is only 16-years-old.

She is still unconscious at home.

My suffering and confusion are one hundred times greater than yours.

Please do not defend your son.

He has done a despicable thing and now must take responsibility.

Do you understand that?

The woman listens as the man speaks without stopping. Doubts cross her mind, but her maternal instincts take over, and she immediately launches into a defense of her son.

THE AMERASIAN'S MOTHER

Why would anyone believe you? Where is your proof?

Are you trying to take advantage of my son?

He has been sponsored to go to America.

In the last few months, many people have come to this house to ask for a favor or to discuss this or that.

I am not new to this.

It won't work, sir!

My son and I will not let anyone take advantage of us.

For years we have had a hard and difficult life, and no one has ever even glanced at us.

Now, suddenly, tons of people are coming to our door to plot this and that.

Do not falsely accuse us. I won't believe you.

The man feels embarrassed and angry that the woman is distrustful and antagonistic toward him. He tries to control his feelings so as to be able to convince her.

THE MAN

Previously, I didn't even know who your son was, or that he had been sponsored to go to the US. However, he has done this thing, and he must take responsibility. You are a mother. You love your son dearly, so I am sure you understand how much I love my daughter especially under these circumstances. I haven't gone to the police because I wanted to talk reason to you first. If both you and your son prove to be irresponsible, I will be forced to bring this matter to the court.

At this point the man sees a new aspect of the issue and emphasizes it.

THE MAN

If this thing becomes a matter of law, your son will be a criminal. Do you think your son can go to America if he has been prosecuted and sentenced?

It is now the woman's turn to become embarrassed and fearful of his reasoning. Suddenly, she feels hatred for this emaciated man who has brought her bad news along with these threats. She feels like screaming.

THE AMERASIAN'S MOTHER

I am not afraid of you. Don't threaten me. My son is innocent. He has committed no crime. Go away. I don't want to listen to you anymore.

Her anger is like a flame. It reignites the anger he has been trying to suppress. He stands up and speaks haltingly.

THE MAN

You... you. So this is your attitude? You son will get a taste of what I can do. That mixed race sex fiend will not escape punishment! Just open your eyes, and you will see what happens!

THE AMERASIAN"S MOTHER

> How dare you threaten me? Get out of here or I will scream for the entire hamlet to hear! Anyone out there…

The man topples the chair as he runs out of the house while the woman holds her face in her hands and then crumbles to the ground.

19. THE BLACK AMERASIAN'S HOME – INSIDE – EVENING

After the departure of the emaciated man, the Amerasian's mother is so tired she can barely drag herself to her bed to rest. She thinks and thinks about the past and reminisces.

20. THE BLACK AMERASIAN'S HOME – INSIDE – EVENING (FLASHBACK)

Scenes of the woman's life with her previous husband. He was an unemployed nobody, a gambler and a drunk, who liked to beat her up.

He died from a stroke while drunk.

21. US MILITARY BARRACK – MORNING (FLASHBACK)

A US military barrack near the township. The barrack is on a treeless hilltop and surrounded by barbed wire. It has a couple of guard towers. Several GIs can be seen walking back and forth.

Some GIs are joking with the Vietnamese women working inside the barrack.

Some GIs are sitting by themselves reading letters from home. Some are crying.

A tall, robust black GI is paying his attention to the mother of the Amerasian. He gives her some canned food and cigarettes. They communicate by gestures.

22. THE HOME OF THE BLACK AMERASIAN'S MOTHER – INSIDE - EVENING (FLASHBACK)

The black GI and the mother of the Amerasian are living in the same house. They have sex on the bed a few times.

23. THE HOME OF THE BLACK AMERASIAN'S MOTHER – OUTSIDE - EVENING (FLASHBACK)

The Black GI and the mother of the Amerasian are saying goodbye to each other in front of the house. He then leaves. She has had no news of him since.

24. THE HOME OF THE BLACK AMERASIAN – INSIDE – DAYTIME

The Amerasian's mother is in her bed and having a hard time sleeping when he returns home with a long face. He becomes agitated when he sees his mother all curled up and having trouble breathing. He rushes to her bedside and asks her:

THE AMERASIAN

> Mother, are you sick? Please tell me what you are suffering from, so that I can get you some medicine.

The mother weakly attempts to sit up and then asks her son to sit on the bed beside her. She looks at his face for a long time and sees that he is sad, as if tormented by something. She suddenly understands that whatever the skinny man has told her is true. She feels as if someone has beaten her with a big stick. She grasps her son's head and speaks weakly.

THE AMERASIAN'S MOTHER

> Why did you do what you did? Your life was going to change for the better, and now all may be lost. Are you crazy?

The Amerasian lifts his head up and looks at his mother.

THE AMERASIAN

> So you know everything?

She nods painfully.

THE AMERASIAN'S MOTHER

> Yes. Her father came here himself to tell me about it. He said that if you do not deal with this matter, he will go to the police. However, tell me the truth. Did you do it or were you seduced by both of them?

The Amerasian speaks as if he were in the confessional.

THE AMERASIAN

I did it. I am the one to blame. Please don't think badly of them. She is still very innocent. I love her, and her parents know nothing about that. It is only because I love her too much. I will go see them, confess, and ask for their forgiveness.

The Amerasian's mother grasps his hand as if she were afraid he would go right away.

THE AMERASIAN'S MOTHER

No, don't do that. That won't do. We need to think this through. You know that if you admit to the crime, you will not be allowed to go to America. Instead, you will go to jail. So the alternative is maybe to deny everything. Were there any witnesses?

The Amerasian is surprised because he hadn't thought of that.

THE AMERASIAN

How can I deny it? I did it myself. I love her and want to marry her later. Her father is right. I did a bad thing and must pay for it.

As she listens to her son talk, mixed feelings rise in her heart. She ends up by comforting him.

THE AMERASIAN

Well, do not torture yourself over this. Nothing is lost yet. But don't go looking for them right away. Let me think first if there are any good solutions.

25. THE SIDEWALK – OUTSIDE – MORNING

The man spreads a sheet of nylon on the sidewalk and goes through the motion of putting out several dozen used books for sale as he does every day. But his mind burns with the desire for revenge for the shame and suffering he has endured. Some people stop by to inquire about the books on display. He doesn't even answer them, and they walk away.

26. THE FARM – OUTSIDE –MORNING (FLASHBACK)

The man is working as a field laborer. He makes a feeble attempt to break the soil with a hoe. The other workers laugh at him and make fun of him because he is so weak.

27. THE STREET CORNER – OUTSIDE –MORNING (FLASHBACK)

The man is selling lottery tickets behind a small sidewalk stand. He looks at the passers-by and despairs that no one is stopping to buy anything from him.

28. THE GIRL'S HOME – OUTSIDE – AFTERNOON

The man takes out an old bayonet and begins to sharpen it on a stone in the garden. The bayonet is a military one. It has a pointed tip, and the edge is sharp.

The sound of the bayonet scratching on the stone cuts into his heart. He sharpens the bayonet with all the force of his pain and hatred. After a while, the bayonet shines like a flash of the setting sun, and its tip is as sharp as that of a lance.

He imagines the bayonet in his bony hand penetrating the heart of the savage Amerasian.

29. THE GIRL'S HOME – INSIDE – AFTERNOON

It is getting dark. The man looks inside the house and sees his daughter trying to sleep in her bed. Her face is pale. He cannot hold back his tears. He whispers to her.

> THE MAN
>
> Don't be sad. I will avenge you.

He leaves the home quietly.

30. THE AMERASIAN'S HOME– OUTSIDE – AFTERNOON

The man approaches the Amerasian's house and then stops to observe. The area where the house is located is rather isolated. The houses are far from each other because they all have large yards. Along the roads are many small bushes. These could prove very useful when plan-ning an ambush.

He stops in front of the house just behind the hibiscus hedge and listens. He hears nothing but silence, and a woman coughing now and then. He quietly hides behind a bush and waits.

He doesn't have to wait long. He hears footsteps and then sees the shadow of a tall, lanky man emerge from the dark-ening sky. The shadow is the same as that of the man he saw when he chased desperately after his daughter's rapist.

Seeing the shadow brings back a vivid image of his daughter writhing in pain on the ground. Hatred flares up in his mind, giving him superhuman strength as he lunges for-ward and thrusts his knife at the Amerasian's chest just as he is approaching a bend in the road.

But the Amerasian's reflex is faster. He is able to deflect the knife with his arm, even though, in the process of doing so, the very sharp blade draws blood as it glances away.

The Amerasian then grabs the old man's hand and pulls him closer so as to punch him in the face. The two men see each other's faces up close in the twilight and recognize each other. The old man screams.

THE MAN

I will kill you, you barbaric Amerasian!

I must kill you!

The Amerasian maintains his iron grip on the man's arm but his eyes appear troubled. He stammers:

THE AMERASIAN

Please... forgive me... I didn't do it intentionally.

I truly love your daughter... I plan to come see you tomorrow...

The Amerasian regains his composure. He gently relaxes his grip. The man is surprised. His anger seems to have left him. He, too, stammers:

THE MAN

What... what did you say? You are in love?

The Amerasian bends down to the man's level since he is about a head taller. He then speaks in a pleading voice.

THE AMERASIAN

Yes. I love your daughter, but I did a bad and unwise thing.

I committed a crime, and I must take responsibility.

I won't run away from it.

My only hope is that you will somehow forgive me and give me a chance to redeem myself.

I want to see her again very much, but I am afraid you won't allow it.

Is she well now?

The man cannot believe what he is hearing with his own ears. In the twilight gloom, the face of the black Amerasian does not look fierce or cruel, does not look remorseful, but rather remorseful and sincere. He is almost on his knees as he says these words. The hatred in the old man's heart suddenly melts as he realizes that the young man is speaking the truth. The old man now speaks in a slow and measured tone.

THE MAN

So, what do you intend to do now?

The Amerasian maintains his near kneeling position.

THE AMERASIAN

I told her that I would marry her in a few years, after I return from America.

However, because of the incident, I will discuss this with my mother and then come to talk to you.

I will not let her down or disappoint you.

THE MAN

(Knitting kis eyebrows)

But your mother already told me otherwise.

He grasps the old man's hand.

THE AMERASIAN

I know.

> But that is because my mother doesn't understand or she just wants to protect me.
>
> My mother is not an unreasonable person.
>
> I will convince her.

The man keeps his gaze fixed on the Amerasian's face as he backs away and melts into the darkness.

The man bends down to pick up the steel bayonet that has fallen to the ground and where it lies gleaming.

He said.

> ## THE MAN
>
> Alright.
>
> I will trust you for now.
>
> Go put a bandage on your arm and then discuss the matter with your mother.
>
> Then both of you come see me tomorrow at 8 AM sharp.
>
> Be there on time. Both of you. At exactly 8 AM.
>
> If you two don't show up, I won't need the law to exact justice.
>
> This bayonet will not spare you.

The man then leaves the scene as the Amerasian walks slowly home.

31. THE GIRL'S HOME – INSIDE –EVENING

The girl is lying in her bed half asleep. Her father walks in, mumbles words to the effect that he will avenge her, and then walks out. Still sleepy, the girl vaguely hears what he says but when she turns her torso to sit up, he is already gone.

She makes an effort to sit up and then silently clasps her hands together to pray and says quietly:

> THE GIRL
>
> I pray that no harm comes his way and that he will come back to me just like he did in previous months.

32. THE GIRL'S HOME – INSIDE – DAYTIME (FLASHBACK)

The girl is pacing aimlessly in the yard in front of her house. She then walks toward the grass field ahead, gazes at the far away mountains, and goes back to sit beside a large tomb in the cemetery.

The girl is standing in front of her father's bookcase. She looks at one book after another, then takes one and reads attentively while sitting on a chair near the window (The book is "Butterfly Soul Dreaming of a Fairy" by Khai Hung).

33. THE CEMETERY – OUTSIDE – AFTERNOON (FLASHBACK)

An intermittent breeze blows in the sunshine. The girl is sitting alone besidea large tomb with a roof. She sees the Amerasian walk into the cemetery from the road. He walks slowly from one tomb to another, stopping now and then as if his mind is elsewhere. Suddenly he sees her sitting by herself at the tomb. He opens his eyes wide and looks into her eyes for a little while and then asks:

> THE AMERASIAN
>
> Why are you sitting here?
>
> THE GIRL
>
> (Pointing in the direction of her home)
>
> My house is nearby, right over there!
>
> THE AMERASIAN
>
> Why aren't you in school?
>
> THE GIRL
>
> My parents let me stay home this year because they are short of money.

The Amerasian moves closer and sits down next to her. He remains quiet for a while and then speaks.

> THE AMERASIAN
>
> What a pity. You are still young and yet you must leave school.

Me too, I left school several years ago to work and help my mother. But I am now a grownup.

Are you sad?

THE GIRL

Of course I am sad. But I have gotten used to it.

THE AMERASIAN

Do you come here often?

THE GIRL

Every now and then. When I have nothing to do.

THE AMERASIAN

Aren't you afraid?

THE GIRL

Of what?

THE AMERASIAN

Ghosts. This is a cemetery after all.

THE GIRL

My home is nearby, so I am used to it. I have never seen a ghost.

THE AMERASIAN

Ok, then when I have time, can I come and play with you?

The girl looks at the Amerasian inquisitively. She doesn't feel fearful of him.

> THE GIRL
>
> Yes, that's fine with me.
>
> THE AMERASIAN
>
> (His face visibly happy)
>
> That would be great! I will be able to see you more often.

34. THE CEMETERY – OUTSIDE – AFTERNOON (FLASHBACK)

The girl is sitting beside the large tomb. The Amerasian comes and sits down next to her, casually and naturally.

> THE GIRL
>
> You are not working today?
>
> THE AMERASIAN
>
> I am, but I missed you too much, so I asked them if I could leave early to see you.
>
> Did you miss me?
>
> THE GIRL
>
> (She lowers her head and mumbles)
>
> I don't know.

THE AMERASIAN

Why not? I missed you terribly. I think about you all the time.

I always want to see you. Everyday.

Are you happy to see me?

THE AMERASIAN

Just say it. Did you miss me? Are you happy to see me sitting here?

The girl just nods gently. The Amerasian gives her shoulder a happy squeeze.

THE AMERASIAN

That is all I want. With you beside me, I want nothing else.

35. THE AMERASIAN'S HOME – INSIDE – EVENING

The Amerasian returns home, bandages his wounds, and is chatting with his mother when someone knocks at the door. It is Policeman A, the officer in charge of the neighborhood where they reside.

A is wearing his uniform and looks commanding. The mother invites A to come in. He sits in a chair, leans backs, looks at the mother and then the son attentively with his small but piercing eyes. He then affects a half smile and speaks.

POLICEMAN A

So, what is up with you two? Why do you look so tired and worried?

Shouldn't you be upbeat now that you are going to America?

The Amerasian's mother manages to crack a smile.

THE AMERASIAN'S MOTHER

It's nothing. I am a little tired and sick these days. I seem to be always sick, what a nuisance.

Policeman A nods.

POLICEMAN A

Right. This kind of weather makes people sick, but a sickness in the head is more worrisome because it can cause people to crumble very quickly. Don't you agree? Perhaps I can help?

The woman sees that Policeman A's attitude presages nothing good, but isn't quite sure what he knows or wants. That makes her a little nervous.

THE AMERASIAN'S MOTHER

I don't think you can cure anything.

Policeman A cracks an enigmatic smile.

POLICEMAN A

But I can. Actually, no one else but me can cure you of

what ails you.

Isn't that true, my mixed race pal?

A looks at the Amerasian and sternly knits his eyebrows.

POLICEMAN A

Well, let's talk seriously. My Amerasian friend, what did you do? Why don't you tell us the truth and nothing but the truth?

The Amerasian appears to be embarrassed and he looks at his mother.

THE AMERASIAN

I... I didn't do anything.

Policeman A lowers his voice and says sharply.

POLICEMAN A

Oh right, you didn't do anything.

If you really don't want people to know what you did, you shouldn't have done it.

If you did it, people will know about it.

If you did an earthshaking thing, how could you expect that no one would find out?

The mother and son duo sit dumbstruck upon hearing the words of Policeman A. The mother tries to mitigate.

THE AMERASIAN'S MOTHER

I don't know what you are talking about.

My son didn't do anything bad.

He is going to America soon, so he would have to be very stupid to do bad things.

POLICEMAN A

And yet he did. I will be straight with you two. Policemen from another neighborhood have started an investigation, and they may be here tomorrow morning. This mixed race boy will be arrested, and you will need to be prepared to bring rice to him in prison. And you can forget about going to America.

THE AMERASIAN'S MOTHER

(Turning white with fear)

Is it true? How could they move so fast? No one has denounced him yet.

Policeman A is surprised, but he catches on quickly.

POLICEMAN A

How do you know no one has denounced him?

Ah, so you did negotiate with them, right?

Even if no one has denounced him, your Amerasian son has committed a crime, and he must be punished.

The law won't forgive him.

> Raping someone under age is punishable by tens of years in prison.
>
> It is not a minor crime.

Policeman A stays silent for a while to let his words sink in and then says softly:

> POLICEMAN A
>
> I know you two are hardworking and law-abiding people. He is also a gentle person.
>
> Now that this is happening, I can help, even though it won't be easy since it involves so many people.

Like a drowning person grasping at a life buoy, the mother speaks hastily.

> THE AMERASIAN'S MOTHER
>
> So you can help us? How much money will it take? I will do my best.
>
> POLICEMAN A
>
> This is a difficult matter. It may take four, five, maybe seven bars of gold, or perhaps more, I don't know yet. But I will do my best.

The woman appears dejected.

> THE AMERASIAN'S MOTHER
>
> That's a lot. I don't see how I can put up that much.
>
> POLICEMAN A

That's your problem.

But both of you are going to America, and there are probably many over there who want to help you.

She holds her head in her hands, turns to her son, and starts sobbing.

THE AMERASIAN'S MOTHER

You are causing me so much pain. I don't know what to do now.

The Amerasian looks at his mother with fearful eyes. He is also startled because he cannot believe that events have moved so fast. He is also embarrassed that he cannot say anything to console his mother.

Coldly, Policeman A stands up.

POLICEMAN A

OK, I am leaving now to let you two discuss things be-tween yourselves. But do remember that this is a very secret matter that you can't discuss with anyone else. I have taken a big risk to talk to you because I want to help you two. But if my superiors hear of this, I can easily lose my rank. There is one thing I want to add: you, half breed, should make yourself scarce for a time, and preferably leave town. If the police catch you, it's over. You should probably leave town tonight because they may come anytime. Do you understand? I'll come back tomorrow to meet you, madam.

The dazed mother and son look on as the policeman walks

out. She keeps still for a moment and then wakes up from her stupor to close the door in a hurry.

36. THE GIRL'S HOME – INSIDE – MORNING

In the morning, as the girl's parents are pacing impatiently outside as they wait for the arrival of the Amerasian and his mother, another man comes.

This man is Policeman B. His arrival surprises them.

Policeman B takes in the entire dilapidated house before stepping into the home and loudly greeting the homeowners, who are sitting in the middle of the living room.

> POLICEMAN B
>
> Hello, sir and madam. You aren't working today?
>
> THE MAN
>
> Hello! Is there anything we can do for you?
>
> POLICEMAN B
>
> I am the neighborhood policeman. I have something to ask you.
>
> THE MAN
>
> Then please step inside.

The girl's father pulls out a short stool from under the wobbly table.

THE MAN

Please, sit here for now. Our home is not too well equipped.

POLICEMAN B

No problem. I understand. How is your business these days?

THE MAN

The same. Just getting by.

POLICEMAN B

You two look sad. Are you worried about something?

Both the man and his wife look startled. The man attempts a faint smile.

THE MAN

No, nothing. We always look like that. Can't buy or sell anything.

Just look around at our home, and you'll understand.

Policeman B looks around the house with an understanding eye. He suddenly notices someone moving on a bed set behind a dirty curtain. He looks at the bed intensely and turns around to ask the man.

POLICEMAN B

Is one of your kids sick?

The man's face turns white.

THE MAN

Yes.

Policeman B attempts to stand up.

POLICEMAN B

Please let me see if I can do anything to help.

The man raises his hand to stop him.

THE MAN

No, there's no need. She just has a slight fever.

Policeman B speaks in a solemn, official tone.

POLICEMAN B

I am here to discuss an important matter with you two. Some people came to inform me that a rape had been committed in this area and that the victim was your daughter. That is a crime that the police must investigate and solve in order to maintain public order and security. Please tell me what you know about this matter.

The father is shocked when he hears Policeman B raise the question. He glances at his wife and responds in a firm voice.

THE MAN

I haven't heard any such story. My daughter doesn't suffer from anything. Those people must have been wrong.

Policeman B knits his brow upon hearing the man's answer. It isn't what he was expecting.

POLICEMAN B

I understand that this matter is very hard to discuss. Everybody would say what you did. No one wants to talk publicly about such matters. However, please think about it and come to the right decision. This is a serious crime, and, moreover, your daughter is the victim. You too should tell the truth.

THE MAN

I already told you that it didn't happen.

Why should I hide anything?

POLICEMAN B

I fully understand this is a sad thing that may cause shame to your family. But consider this. The criminal must be punished, and your daughter must be compensated. Why should you be disadvantaged when the bad guy is free to roam above the law? If such criminals go unpunished, crime will spread.

THE MAN

I understand that. But the thing didn't happen, so how can I say otherwise?

POLICEMAN B

You two don't make sense. Why are you protecting the criminal? No matter what, your daughter already has a bad reputation because people in the neighborhood are talking. I know you are an intellectual, so you should behave in a logical way.

As he hears the word "intellectual", an anger flares up in the man's mind. He raises his voice.

THE MAN

What is the point of being an intellectual? An intellectual still has to use a hoe, sell used books, and work as a laborer. Please stop calling me an intellectual.

POLICEMAN B

That is another story. What we are dealing with here is the application of the law, the punishment of the guilty, the upholding of law and order, and the removal of bad elements from the neighborhood.

THE MAN

Please stop lecturing us about real life. How many criminals, how many corrupt officials who oppress the people are out walking around without anyone punishing them? We, the lowly people, are the only ones suffering.

Suddenly the conversation veers into a different direction. Policeman B starts to feel hot under his collar.

POLICEMAN B

Be careful what you say. The state never forgives the bad. There are countless resolutions, proclamations, and trials aimed at eradicating the bad. All societies are the same: next to the bad or negative is the good or positive. But we must be able to tell the difference between substance and phenomena...

THE MAN

You don't need to lecture us on resolutions. I have heard too much about them. The problem is what happens in real life, in the real society. What is the essen-tial nature? What is a phenomenon? All these are just figures of speech. Many phenomena become essential nature. Essential nature gives rise to the phenomena. You won't be able to convince anyone going that route speaking that way.

Policeman B is surprised at the man's reaction, and he decides not to give in.

POLICEMAN B

Alright, if necessary, we will discuss these matters further later, when we have more time. But to get back to the matter at hand, you know well that the rapist is a black Amerasian, so how can you not feel full of shame and hate? Previously, the Americans invaded our country, committed countless crimes, and now their remnants still commit crimes and are hellbent on destroying our country. I will tell you this truth: No matter how much you want to protect him, I will do my best to bring this to light and him to justice, so that he can be punished. I will never let him get away.

37. A RURAL VILLAGE – OUTSIDE – EVENING (FLASH-BACK)

A group of American soldiers are firing indiscriminately at civilians – mostly women and children – during a sweep of the village. Houses with straw roofs are on fire. Tree branches are broken. A helicopter circles overhead.

After the American soldiers withdraw, Policeman B, in black guerilla garb, runs into the village. He turns over the dead bodies to look at their faces. He grasps the body of a girl and bursts into wailing tears.

38. THE GIRL'S HOME – INSIDE – MORNING (CONTINUED)

Blood rushes to the man's face.

> THE MAN
>
> There are no wars without crimes, and both sides in a war commit them. I say so, not to defend the American imperialists, but because we must be fair when judging history. We must find the true cause of the war. It is obvious the imperialist countries had their own ambitions. The Americans did. So did the Russians. Both the US and the USSR funded the Vietnam War because it was also their war. The Vietnamese people, on the other hand, were themselves divided, and they invited foreign troops and arms to come into the country to massacre each other. No matter what the reasons and the ideals offered to justify the war, the true nature of the war is the same. You may say I am a reactionary, but I say it

all the same because to me it is the truth. Before, we "fought against the Americans to save the country", but now we are begging them to normalize diplomatic and commercial relations. Some people even say we are "inviting the Americans in to save the country". What does that say about the meaning of all the sacrifices this country has endured?

Policeman B is disconcerted as he listens to the man's ramblings and the lack of regard for him when he tries to open his mouth to insert a comment. In the end, he can take it no longer and raises his arm and voice to speak.

POLICEMAN B

All right, let's stop arguing. These are big issues, and we can debate them later. This is not to say that I think you're right. But what we are discussing now is the rape crime committed by the black Amerasian…

THE MAN

I don't know if the black Amerasian did or did not commit a rape crime. But I know that being black is not a crime. He is innocent, and he deserves our pity when two types of blood course through his veins and, as a result, society despises and isolates him. The war is the real criminal. He didn't ask to be born in this country. To hate him is wrong. Moreover, the fact that he was born is not a crime.

Policeman B is surprised by the man's attitude. He smiles wryly.

POLICEMAN B

I know exactly why you are defending the black Amerasian. He is going to be sponsored to go to America. So is it true that he has promised something to you, so that you will remain silent and accept that your daughter will be disadvantaged? You are so pitiful.

THE MAN (his eyes glowering)

Do not insult me. You are here to investigate, not to teach me a lesson. If you defame me, I will sue you. Even the police must obey the law and respect the people. Are you done? I have nothing else to say.

Policeman B stands up reluctantly.

POLICEMAN B

All right. Fine. Today you are a little upset, and so it is difficult to carry on a conversation. I will come back another day when you are calmer and more composed. Please rest assured that I will get to the bottom of this.

Policeman B glances at the person lying on the bed behind the curtain before walking out of the empty and dilapidated house.

39. THE CEMETERY – OUTSIDE – NIGHT

The Amerasian moves quickly in the dark night. He is as fast as a leopard. His black face and dark clothes allow him to blend into the darkness.

His steps automatically take him to the cemetery near the girl's house, and he makes his way to the large tomb where he and the girl used to sit and talk. He sits there for a very long time and then lies down to sleep.

40. THE CEMETERY – OUTSIDE – NIGHT – A DREAM

Midnight. A crescent moon shines weakly on the world below . The Amerasian looks toward the girl's home and suddenly sees a small, white shadow slowly walking out. The white shadow continues to move slowly toward the tomb and when it gets close, he recognizes the girl. He is so happy and almost screams with joy as he rushes out to greet her. The girl embraces him, and he holds her so tight that he almost suffocates her. Then he carries her to the tomb.

He sits down at the familiar spot while still holding her as if she were a little girl. He bends his head down to her pale face and whispers:

> THE AMERASIAN
>
> I am so sorry. I am so sorry. I should be punished a thousand times.

The girl blinks and smiles. Her voice is weak.

> THE GIRL
>
> I am no longer angry at you. I understand. I'm fine. I will get over it.

He holds her tighter as if afraid she will vanish.

THE AMERASIAN

You mean it? You are no longer angry at me? I was so afraid. I was afraid you would never forgive me, and we would never meet again. The last two days I was very worried, and I missed you terribly, but I was still afraid to go see you again.

The girl lifts one of his large hands from her body and puts it against her face. She speaks softly as if exhaling.

THE GIRL

I miss you, too, and I am also worried about you. My parents are really angry about what happened, and I am afraid my father will seek revenge.

As the rough skin of his hand touches her naïve and sweet face, a wave of happiness hits him. He tries to calm her.

THE AMERASIAN

You don't have to worry too much. I have met your father. In the beginning, he was very angry. But later, he seemed to understand our situation, and I promised that tomorrow morning my mother and I would come meet your parents and talk. I hope your mother will for-give me and allow me to redeem myself.

The girl's eyes glisten under the feeble moonlight.

THE GIRL

Is it true? I am so happy. But how are you going to redeem yourself?

Tiêu Dao Bảo Cự

THE AMERASIAN

I don't know yet. It all depends on your father and mother. Perhaps I will ask to marry you right away, or perhaps I will go to America for a few years, study some more, get a stable job, and when conditions permit, come back for you. What do you think?

THE GIRL

But right now I am too young. How can I marry you?

THE AMERASIAN

Why not? We need to be together, don't you want that?

THE GIRL

(Mumbling, as if talking to herself)

Yes. Yes, I do want that..

THE AMERASIAN

(Thinks for a little while)

Or maybe I don't go to America. I stay here to marry you. I don't need anything else. You are all I need.

The girl looks at him tenderly.

THE GIRL

If necessary, you can go. I will wait for you. I believe you will come back for me. You will come back, won't you?

THE AMERASIAN

Yes. Yes. I will surely come back. I won't leave you alone.

The Amerasian feels full of happiness. He bends his head down and kisses the girl on her lips. She kisses him back. It is the first real kiss of his life, and he is totally absorbed in it.

The girl suddenly pushes him away gently.

THE GIRL

Let's take a walk. I want to take me for a walk with me to the grassy hill over there.

He wakes up from his dream.

THE AMERASIAN

If you want to go, I will take you with me. I am ready to do anything you want.

He lifts her up and then guides her to the small road. He puts his arm around her shoulders, and she wraps hers around his waist. Both walk slowly and quietly toward the hill behind her home.

The hill on which the grass grows unevenly because the earth there is not fertile takes on a mysterious sheen under the faint moonlight. A massive black mountain faraway stands out against the night sky. The two keep walking. Now and then they stumble on a mound that causes them to falter and grab each other even tighter. The girl laughs heartily as if having fun in a childish game.

Suddenly, screams from behind are heard.

> Stop! You, the Amerasian, stop!

Startled, the girl and the Amerasian stop dead in their tracks and turn around to look. Three or four people rush out from the back of the girl's house to pursue them. The Amerasian sees some policemen's hats. He takes the girl's hand and pulls her to run away.

THE AMERASIAN

> We have to run.
>
> The police are chasing me.

The two run swiftly down the hill in the direction of the mountain. They stumble and nearly fall several times, but keep running. Their pursuers also keep up with the chase. Now and then, their call to "stop" reverberates in the air. Suddenly a shot rings out like a thunder clap in the dark and empty night.

The girl lets out a scream and collapses. The Amerasian turns to pick up the girl, but sees blood on her back. In a panic, he lifts her up and keeps running, while attempting to speak to her between heavy breaths.

THE AMERASIAN

> Don't, don't die on me. I will… take you with me.…

He can tell that she is still bleeding. Her blood feels warm as it spreads over the hand that is holding her.

Another shot rings out. He feels a sharp pain in his back, and his chest explodes as if it had been torn apart. He falls face down with his arms still tightly holding on to the girl.

The two fall and tumble down into a deep ditch at the foot of the hill. He feels weightless and then feels pain as his head crashes down on a very hard object. The girl is ejected from his arms and lands on the ground at some distance from him.

41. THE CEMETERY – OUTSIDE – NIGHT

The Amerasian suddenly awakes. He is drenched in sweat. He opens his eyes and tries to look around. He sees that he had fallen asleep at the tomb with his head wedged against a headstone. That is what caused him to have this piercing headache. And the beautiful and terribly frightening scene he just experienced was only a dream.

42. THE AMERASIAN'S HOME – INSIDE – DAYTIME

Policeman A walks into the house without knocking when he sees the Amerasian's mother sitting by herself in the middle of the house. She coughs and looks sad. Her eyes are sunken.

Policeman A greets her and looks around.

> POLICEMAN A
>
> Greetings. How are you? Where is the Amerasian?

The woman answers without looking at Policeman A.

THE AMERASIAN'S MOTHER

He is gone.

Policeman A pulls a chair out to sit on without waiting to be asked.

POLICEMAN A

So, what have you two decided?

The woman suddenly turns toward him, grabs his hand, and begins to plead:

THE AMERASIAN'S MOTHER

Please help me. He is my only son. Please have pity on him. He is not a bad boy.

Policeman A taps her hand gently.

POLICEMAN A

Rest assured. I already promised. I understand young folks like him are just restless.

THE AMERASIAN'S MOTHER

(exhaling)

My son and I have met the girl's father. He understands the situation and appears to be sympathetic. He is unlikely to denounce my son. Furthermore, my son knows the girl; she is not a stranger. He even loves her.

Policeman A's eyes widen upon hearing these new revelations.

POLICEMAN A

Is that true? Then there is little to worry about. The issue is the police. I understand our hamlet has a policeman who really hates the Amerasian, and he has decided to punish him. If this matter is reported to the higher-ups, it will become more complicated.

THE AMERASIAN'S MOTHER

You already promised to help us, so please do right by us. I won't forget your help.

POLICEMAN A

It's fine with me. But you must remember I can't do all of it alone. You do understand all but too well that there are others, and the higher-ups, too.

THE AMERASIAN'S MOTHER

 will do my best, but you must understand that our resources are limited.

POLICEMAN A (smiling

What's there to worry about? You are going to America. Going to America these days is like going to heaven, don't you know that?

THE AMERASIAN'S MOTHER

It is my fate to be miserable. I will stay miserable all my life

Policeman A wants to say something, but suddenly someone walks into the courtyard. That someone is Policeman B. The two policemen salute each other. Policeman B greets the woman and then turns around to ask Policeman A.

POLICEMAN B

Investigating? Found anything yet?

POLICEMAN A

Ah… I am only visiting….

POLICEMAN B

OK, can I talk to the lady of the house for a moment?

POLICEMAN A

No problem…Make yourself at home…

POLICEMAN B

I am a policeman from the nearby hamlet. My responsibility in coming here is to ask you a few questions. The woman looks at Policeman B and is frightened by his austere and serious look. She mumbles:

THE AMERASIAN'S MOTHER

You…you…what do you want to ask about?

POLICEMAN B

A rape occurred ina nearby hamlet, which is under my jurisdiction. The people came to me and told me that the culprit was your son, the mixed-race kid. So where is he now?

As he asks the question, Policeman B scrutinizes the woman's confused face.

THE AMERASIAN'S MOTHER

He is at work.

POLICEMAN B

Where does he work? When will he be back?

THE AMERASIAN'S MOTHER

I don't know for sure. He goes off with his friends. Sometimes he goes off for a few days.

POLICEMAN B

Did your son tell you anything about the rape?

THE AMERASIAN'S MOTHER

No. My son is a good boy. He doesn't do bad things. Please don't speak ill of him without cause.

POLICEMAN B

You should know, madam, that rape is a crime, and an even more serious crime when the victim is underage. The police will never forgive, and the law will punish the culprit severely. However, if the culprit repents and turns himself in, he will receive some leniency. Our system treats those who run away from us much more harshly than those who run to us. If he turns himself in and confesses, the sentence will be lighter. I heard that the two of you have been sponsored to go to America. If this problem is not cleared up, how will you two be able to go? If you love your son, ask him to turn himself in. Hiding will only harm him. Do you agree?

The mother tries to stay calm, but she acts as if she were angry.

THE AMERASIAN'S MOTHER

What are you talking about? My son is innocent and yet he has to confess? What does that mean? We aren't afraid, and my son doesn't need to hide anywhere. Please don't try to scare us. It is useless.

Policeman A, who has been listening to the two of them from the beginning, now interjects.

POLICEMAN A

Policeman B, I have also heard some rumors about the rape at your hamlet, but maybe it doesn't have anything to do with the Amerasian. I am responsible for this area. I know the Amerasian has always been a good boy. He has never done anything wrong or disturbed the peace in any way. All he did was to work to earn a living and support his mother. You really should investigate more before accusing an innocent person unjustly.

Surprised, Policeman B opens his eyes wide and looks at Policeman A.

POLICEMAN B

Why are you even saying this? Are you trying to defend him? Our duty is to apply the law strictly, so as not to condemn the innocent or to let the guilty escape justice. Even if he was a good boy in the past,, if he commits a crime now, he must be punished.

POLICEMAN A

(laughing dryly)

So you think I don't know that? What proof do you have to come here questioning people? Why didn't you agree to coordinate the matter with the local police, us? Aren't we responsible for this area? Don't you think we know what we are doing?

Policeman B is taken aback by Policeman A's attitude. He responds.

POLICEMAN B

I am only conducting a preliminary investigation. Obviously, we will coordinate with you when we have solid leads. And I trust that you will cooperate with us to ex-pedite the resolution of this case.

POLICEMAN A

(Looking serious now)

We must apply the law strictly, but we cannot abuse it to harass the people. Without proof and a court's judgment, we cannot consider anyone guilty. Additionally, this mother and her son are about to be sponsored to go to America in accordance with the policy of the government and the agreement between the two countries. This is a big deal, and one can't just do anything one wants to jeopardize relations between the two countries. You must be careful. This is no small matter.

Confused, Policeman B attempts to respond.

POLICEMAN B

What are you talking about? I am only…

Policeman A interrupts him decisively.

POLICEMAN A

Or perhaps you have other reasons to come here to harass them? Please remember I am the one who has jurisdiction over this area, and not you.

B is thoroughly upset now, but he contains his anger as the situation doesn't seem to be in his favor.

POLICEMAN B

Ok, fine. If I find proof, he won't be able to escape me. And remember this: whoever attempts to protect him will also be held responsible.

Policeman B then pushes the chair back and walks out.

43. THE GIRL'S HOME – OUTSIDE – AFTER DARK

The Amerasian walks along the edge of the forest to the mountain near the girl's home. He waits until dusk to find a way to meet the girl. He makes himself small to be able to sit inside a rocky cavity like a beast.

When darkness sets in, he leaves the rocky cavity and stealthily moves toward the girl's house.

He presses his head against a crack in the wall of the house. He sees the girl cleaning up something inside. He calls her in a very low voice.

> THE AMERASIAN
>
> Hi, I'm here. Come out and talk to me, please.

The girl is surprised, and she perks her ears up to listen. She stands still for a moment and then silently walks around toward the back of the house to meet him. The Amerasian sees her face: pale and slightly greenish. He takes her hand and leads her to a tree behind the house. She follows him silently. He helps her sit down against the tree. Her head is bent, and she says nothing. He holds her hand tightly and speaks earnestly.

> THE AMERASIAN
>
> I am so sorry. I did something bad and unforgivable. But please understand that it was because I love you too much.

The girl still doesn't speak. Her silence scares him deeply.

> THE AMERASIAN
>
> I acted so badly. I am sure your parents will never forgive me. I don't know what to do to earn your forgiveness. Please tell me what you are thinking, what you

want. But don't stay silent because that hurts me and makes me suffer. Maybe I should turn myself in so that I can receive a punishment commensurate with my crime. Do you want me to do that? Just say so. I am ready.

The girl slowly lifts her head to look at him. She smiles faintly.

THE GIRL

Don't be afraid. I am not angry at you. I understand.

Her voice is very weak. This is the first time she has opened her mouth in the last few days. The Amerasian is so deeply moved he starts shaking. He grasps her shoulders tightly with his arm.

THE AMERASIAN

Thank you, thank you so much. Only you understand me. Now that you understand, I am no longer worried. Are you well now?

THE GIRL

I am recovering. Nothing serious.

THE AMERASIAN

Oh God! Do you know that last night, when I was sleeping at the tomb, I dreamed about you, and you told me what you just said exactly, word for word. Isn't that wonderful? But later, the police were chasing us and you…you…

He dares not tell her how the dream ended. The girl asks him.

THE GIRL

What happened to me?

THE AMERASIAN

Um... ah... you suddenly disappeared.

He changes the story quickly, so as not to make her unhappy. The girl suddenly remembers something.

THE GIRL

Why did you wait until now to get in touch with me? Were the police looking for you?

THE AMERASIAN

How did you know?

THE GIRL

I was lying in bed when I overheard a policeman questioning my parents. He threatened to arrest you. I was very worried for you.

THE AMERASIAN

Right. I also heard that rumor, and that's why I am hiding now. I actually promised your father that my mother and I would come to your house to talk, but before that could happen, I had to run and hide. Please tell your

> parents why I had to do what I did, please apologize to them on my behalf, and tell them that when the right moment comes, I will come back to meet them. Do you believe me?

The girl gazes intently into the Amerasian's face even as it fades into the darkness of the night. She whispers.

> THE GIRL
>
> I believe you. I will wait for you.

"Oh God, just like in my dream!," he whispers softly and bends down to kiss her, but then hears a voice coming from the front of the house, saying,

> "It's dark, why don't you turn on the light?"
>
> THE AMERASIAN
>
> All right, I must go now. I will come back another time. Please wait for me.

He kisses her gently on the forehead and then runs toward the grassy hill and quickly disappears.

44. THE GIRL'S HOME – OUTSIDE – NIGHT

Wrapped in his overcoat and with his short gun slung over his shoulder, Policeman B lies in ambush outside the girl's house for 3 nights. He hopes to catch a glimpse of the Amerasian, but it is all in vain. He sees the moon rise and set on three consecutive nights as he waits with some trepidation, but without losing patience. He visualizes in his head the tall silhouette of the Amerasian, and his hatred for the Americans surges again.

45. THE MY LAI MEMORIAL SHRINE - OUTSIDE - DAYTIME (FLASHBACK)

Policeman B stops to watch a few Americans, former soldiers in the Vietnam War, visiting and burning incense at a memorial for civilians massacred during that war.

He walks toward a ditch that had been dug in the ground of the memorial site to serve as a symbol of past events. He remembers his mother, siblings, and all the relatives who were murdered many years ago. His face hardens, and his mind fills with hatred.

46. THE GIRL'S HOME – INSIDE – NIGHT

When the man walks back into the house to turn the light on, he sees his daughter walk in from the back of the house. He is surprised.

> **THE MAN**
>
> Where did you go?

> THE GIRL
>
> I went outside to get some fresh air.

The father grabs a couple of chairs, sets it up under the veranda and asks the girl to sit down to talk with him. The girl is still weak but her face has brightened even though it is still pale. The light from the rising moon weakly brightens the yard in front of the veranda. He asks with a soft voice.

> THE MAN
>
> Do you feel better now?
>
> THE GIRL
>
> Yes, I do.
>
> THE MAN
>
> Do you blame me and Mother?
>
> THE GIRL
>
> No. Don't be sad. It's not your fault.

The man holds his daughter's head against his shoulder.

> THE MAN
>
> You are so good. You act as if the one needing consolation is not you, but your daddy. We love you very much, but we don't know what to do next.

The girl buries her head in her father's chest.

> THE GIRL

> I know. I will never blame you two.

He caresses his daughter's hair. Suddenly the girl looks up at him.

> THE GIRL
>
> Dad. The Amerasian said he wants to apologize to you two.
>
> THE MAN (taken aback)
>
> What? He came here?
>
> THE GIRL
>
> Yes. He saw me just moments ago. He said he promised to come see both of you, but he can't do it now because the police are pursuing him. He will definitely come back when he can.

The man looks at her inquisitively.

> THE MAN
>
> You don't hate him?

The girl shakes her head gently.

> THE GIRL
>
> No. The Amerasian is not a bad person. He loves me and has admitted that he was wrong.
>
> THE MAN
>
> So how do you treat him?

THE GIRL

I... I also... like him... very much.

The man opens his eyes wide to look at his daughter sitting next to him. The girl lowers her head. Her long black hair covers her innocent face. He asks her as if he is merely curious.

THE MAN

How long have you known him?

THE GIRL

Probably a little more than 3 months.

THE MAN

What do you talk about when you're together?

THE MAN

Did he come to the house or meet you somewhere else?

THE GIRL

We walk on the grassy hill behind the house or sit beside a big tomb in the cemetery.

THE MAN

Has he forced you to do anything against your will?

THE GIRL

No, not at all.

THE MAN

Has he told you that he is being sponsored to go to America?

THE GIRL

Yes. He said he would go there to study and then come back in a few years to marry me, when I am grown up.

THE MAN

Do you believe him?

THE GIRL

Yes. I believe he would never lie to me, and I will wait for him.

The man is surprised when he hears the girl say what she believes so strongly and naturally. He looks at her for a long time and then holds her tightly to comfort her.

THE MAN

My poor daughter. I hope good things will come to you, and you will not have a hard life like your parents.

47. THE AMERASIAN'S HOME – INSIDE – DAYTIME

Policeman A returns to the home of the Amerasian's

mother. As usual, he starts speaking loudly from the outside courtyard.

POLICEMAN A

Are you home, Madam? How come the door is closed during the day, so that the house is dark inside?

The Amerasian's mother opens the door to let Policeman A in. She nods silently in greeting. Each takes a chair to sit on. Policeman A speaks in a low and conspiratorial voice.

POLICEMAN A

I want you to know that the police from the nearby hamlet have a plan to capture the Amerasian, and they are executing it aggressively. The most active one is Policeman B, who came here the other day. He swears he will capture the Amerasian by whatever means necessary. I also know that he has asked the police in nearby hamlets to help him, so the situation is getting very tense. By the way, has the Amerasian returned home in the last few days or has he sent any news?

The mother looks very worried. She exhales.

THE AMERASIAN'S MOTHER

He hasn't come back and hasn't sent any message either. I am so worried.

POLICEMAN A

The police from the nearby hamlet have asked the police from this hamlet to officially coordinate the investigation, but I was able to put a stop to that. I told them that I was responsible for this area and that as far as I knew, I had no indication that he was guilty of anything. However, I can't continue to protect him forever.

The Amerasian's mother is taken aback and she manages to blurt out:

THE AMERASIAN'S MOTHER

So...so...now what can we do?

POLICEMAN A

What can we do now? Don't you know that now we will need to start the process all over again from the beginning?

Policeman A smiles slyly and somewhat sarcastically as she asks innocently:

THE AMERASIAN'S MOTHER

What do you mean, start the process from the beginning?

POLICEMAN A

What I mean to say is "where is the money". Don't you know that? You are really naïve.

Policeman A laughs out loud. The woman understands now and asks earnestly:

THE AMERASIAN'S MOTHER

So how much do I have to pay now?

POLICEMAN A

Three gold bars. For now. More later as needed. We will address the need as it arises.

THE AMERASIAN'S MOTHER

I must give it to you now?

POLICEMAN A

Yes. The car has started to move. Without gas and oil, how else can I make it run?

THE AMERASIAN'S MOTHER

(Dejectedly)

Please wait a moment.

She gets up and walks to the bedroom as Policeman A walks to the gate to look out in all directions and then walks back. He leaves the door ajar. A moment later, the woman comes out of the bedroom and places three gold bars on the table. The gold is carefully wrapped in plastic. She hes-itates a little and then mumbles:

THE AMERASIAN'S MOTHER

Do you give a receipt?

POLICEMAN A

(Arching his eyebrows)

What receipt? If you don't trust me, then let's stop now. I am refueling, so I can't give you a receipt.

THE AMERASIAN'S MOTHER

(Sadly)

Ok, I will have to trust you since there is nothing else I can do.

But you must keep your promise to help my son overcome this difficulty.

If he can truly avoid it, I won't have any regrets, even if it is very expensive.

She says this, but as she watches Policeman A take the three gold bars and put them in his pocket, she feels a sharp pain in her heart. Policeman A pretends to be concerned.

POLICEMAN A

There is no other way. This must be done.

I am sure I will be able to help you.

You and your son are going to America; there is nothing to worry about.

Policeman A then says goodbye to the woman and walks out, leaving her standing in the middle of the room, dazed and fearful that she might lose her gold for nothing.

48. THE GIRL'S HOME – INSIDE – NOON

Noon. Policeman B suddenly enters the girl's house when her parents aren't there.

> **POLICEMAN B**
>
> Hi, kid. Let me ask you a couple of questions.

Surprised, the girl looks out and recognizes the man. She moves back a step as if assuming a defensive position and replies in a harsh voice.

> **THE GIRL**
>
> What do you want?

> **POLICEMAN B**
>
> I just want to ask a few questions, that's all.

> **THE GIRL**
>
> I don't know anything. My parents aren't here. Please wait for my parents to come back.

> **POLICEMAN B**
>
> All I want is to ask you some questions. Nothing serious. Don't be afraid.

> **THE GIRL**
>
> I am not afraid of anything

> **POLICEMAN B**
>
> Then it's good. All I want to do is to help you, I don't have any bad intentions.

He steps inside and automatically pulls out a small chair to sit on.

POLICEMAN B

Please sit down.

The girl remains standing and stares at the policeman. He tries to smile so as to seem friendly.

POLICEMAN B

You don't have to be so tense.

I am just asking a few questions and not trying to harm you.

So, have you recovered?

The girl doesn't answer. He tries to speak softly.

POLICEMAN B

I know you just had a scary experience.

I am sure you are very sad, but all wounds eventually heal.

The point is, you should not be disadvantaged.

Even though you are still young, I am sure you understand what I am trying to say.

THE GIRL

I don't understand what you are saying.

POLICEMAN B

Do you hate him?

THE GIRL

Hate whom?

POLICEMAN B

The Amerasian. The one who hurt you.

THE GIRL

He didn't do anything to hurt me.

Policeman B's eyes brighten. So this girl is tacitly admitting her relationship with the Amerasian. He asks carefully.

POLICEMAN B

So the Amerasian is very good to you?

THE GIRL

Yes.

POLICEMAN B

Does he come here often?

The girl shudders and becomes defensive at this question. She doesn't answer because she now understands why Policeman B has come. Policeman B speaks as if trying to explain something.

POLICEMAN B

Do you know that there are a lot of bad people these days, especially among the young men?

They don't have a job; they don't want to study or work; they gather to play cards, drink, tease girls; and sometimes, they do very bad things. For example, the Amerasian...

The girl reacts immediately.

THE GIRL

The Amerasian didn't do anything bad.

CEMAN B

How do you know? You can't possibly know everything he has done. And speaking of what he did to you, don't you think it was bad? Didn't your parents explain to you what he did?

The girl speaks in a firm voice, her eyes gleaming with trust.

THE GIRL

The Amerasian didn't do anything bad. He loves me.

Policeman B is totally surprised by her reply. He freezes for an instant and then mutters:

POLICEMAN B

Love. So it's love. But you know nothing about love.

You have been used, but you just don't understand, that's all. Poor you.

THE GIRL

It is you who doesn't understand. How could you? All you want to do is to arrest him. You won't succeed.

Policeman B doesn't dare express his anger. He tries to gently explain his position, but the girl doesn't want to hear any of it. He feels like he is losing ground and, dejected, decides to leave the house.

49. THE GIRL'S HOME – OUTSIDE – AFTER DARK

Evening. The girl becomes restless as her intuition tells her the Amerasian will come looking for her. She works, while keeping an ear open, and, sure enough, she hears someone whistling behind the house. She quickly goes out.

The Amerasian greets and embraces her effusively. The two hold on to each other, listen to each other's heartbeats, and then the Amerasian takes her by the hand and guides her toward the grassy hill in the distance.

The sky grows darker. The two sit on the grass, facing the mountain top. No one is around, but the Amerasian still whispers.

> THE AMERASIAN
>
> I miss you so much. I wanted to come back and see you in a few days, but I couldn't wait that long.
>
> So I'm here to see you, even if only for five or ten min-utes.

The girl speaks in an even lower voice.

THE GIRL

Please be careful. The policeman who came to our house earlier returned.

He questioned me and was trying to get news about you.

THE AMERASIAN

What did you say, and did he threaten you?

THE GIRL

How could he threaten me?

I told him you were not a bad person and that you loved me.

THE AMERASIAN

You dared say that?

THE GIRL

Yes, I did. There is nothing to be afraid of.

The Amerasian feels heartened. He squeezes her hand.

THE AMERASIAN

So, you do love me?

The girl hesitates a little.

THE GIRL

Yes... I miss you. I want you to come.

Is that love?

THE AMERASIAN

Yes, that is love. I feel the same for you. Loving each other is not a crime.

Why be afraid?

THE GIRL

But don't… do what you did… that thing… again. I am still very young.

THE AMERASIAN

I wouldn't dare try again. But…may I kiss you?

The girl says nothing. The Amerasian lifts her chin and kisses her gently on the lips. She doesn't know how to kiss him back. Her fingers claw at his arms, and she trembles. The Amerasian stops because he doesn't want to frighten her even though he really wants to bite the plump, moist lips. He says tenderly:

THE AMERASIAN

We will give each other everything when you grow up. I will wait. And you do the same.

THE GIRL

What about your trip to America? Are you still going?

THE AMERASIAN

(Thoughtfully)

The reasons I'm going are to study, get a job, and get to

know my father's homeland.

After all, I also have American blood in my veins.

If nothing stands in the way, I'll go, but if you want me to stay, I will. What do you think?

The girl doesn't answer. She changes the subject.

THE GIRL

In the past, why did your father come here?

THE AMERASIAN

Because of the war. He was in the military, so he had to come here.

According to my mother, he didn't like fighting, and he never killed anyone.

He was very kind and wanted to live peacefully with my mother.

THE GIRL

And after that, where did he go?

THE AMERASIAN

His unit was moved to another location, and he lost track of my mother. She didn't know if he had died or gone home.

I never got to see him because he left while I was still in my mother's belly.

I have a photo of him and my mother.

He was very handsome.

Oh, and I also heard that your father used to be a school teacher.

How come he doesn't teach anymore?

THE GIRL

I don't know.

Perhaps it is because my grandfather was a South Vietnamese officer who died in battle, while my father was a teacher who didn't get along with the principal and thus was fired.

My father loves me very much.

It is so sad that he has to work so hard to support the family.

THE AMERASIAN

The war ended a long time ago. Our parents suffered, yet we continue to suffer.

It just doesn't make sense to me. If I don't go to America, I will just be a laborer, working here and there to support you.

Are you OK with that?

THE GIRL

Yes, I am used to hardship. I don't need a lot.

But if you go to America, your future will be brighter, right?

THE AMERASIAN

I'm not sure, but I hope so.

I heard that the US government would pay for the education of people like me.

THE GIRL

Then you should go. I can wait for you.

THE AMERASIAN

What if I can't come back?

THE GIRL

Your karma would catch up with you. But I believe you will come back, right?

THE AMERASIAN

I'm only joking. I will come back for sure.

The Amerasian holds the girl tightly against him. Dreamily, the two share their body warmth. The moon rises, and the wind begins to blow. The girl suddenly becomes agitated.

THE GIRL

Stop. I must go back. My father is probably home. Oh, and I already told him that you had apologized for not coming with your mother.

THE AMERASIAN

What did he say?

THE GIRL

He seemed to understand. But he doesn't think we are in love.

THE AMERASIAN

In time he will understand.

50. THE GRASSY HILL – OUTSIDE – AFTER DARK

The girl stands up and then pulls the Amerasian up, too. Arm in arm, they walk toward the girl's home. The wind blows and lifts up her hair, exposing her white face, which contrasts with the dark skin of the Amerasian.

The two lovers walk as if in a dream. They aren't aware that Policeman B, who has been lying in ambush behind her house with a gun, has his eyes trained on them.

The lovers' shadows are clearly outlined against the sky. The tall, lanky Amerasian walks alongside the thin, frail girl. At times, the two shadows merge, and then separate.

POLICEMAN B

These two are really in love. Wait! What did I just think? Did I accept that they were in love? This can't be. She was seduced.

He keeps his gun aimed at the couple.

POLICEMAN B

(thinking silently)

Do I have the right to shoot them? No. All I want is to arrest them. But for what reason? And it might not be that easy. He is twice my size and twice as strong. Without a gun it would be difficult for me to subdue him. I don't have my handcuffs with me. What should I do? Hm, this is going to be complicated.

The shadows keep getting nearer and nearer. Policeman B aims his gun at the Amerasian's chest and then subconsciously lowers it to his legs. The Amerasian and the girl are now just a few feet away from him. He can hear their footsteps. Unsure about what he should do, he watches the Amerasian bend down to kiss the girl on the cheek and then quickly turn around and run away and disappear like an illusion on the grassy hill, bathed in dim moonlight.

Policeman B rubs his eyes as if he has just awoken from a dream-filled sleep. He lies very still to let the girl pass without seeing him and then gets up, wipes his clothes clean with his hand, exhales deeply, and silently retreats.

51. POLICEMAN B'S HOME – INSIDE – NIGHT

After Policeman B arrives home andis changing his clothes, a thought suddenly flashes through his mind. It occurs to him that the Amerasian will stop by his mother's home to visit her after seeing his girlfriend. If so, Policeman B can catch him there, and this time, he won't be able to escape. So Policeman B hurriedly puts back on his uniform, grabs a pair of handcuffs, and sets off for the Amerasian's home.

52. THE HOME OF THE AMERASIAN'S MOTHER – OUTSIDE – INSIDE – AFTERNOON

Stealthily, Policeman B approaches the house and puts his ear to the door to listen. The door is closed. There is a light on inside the house, and he can hear the sound of people talking. He immediately recognizes the voice of Policeman A and that of the Amerasian's mother. There is a third voice, and he realizes that it must be the Amerasian's. Without thinking, he pushes the door open and walks in. Startled, the three people in the house turn toward the door. Policeman B rejoices as he now sees that the third person in the house is indeed the Amerasian.

The Amerasian is rattled. Luckily, because he is black, the color doesn't drain from his face. Instead, his eyes open wide, and his mouth gapes, showing his white teeth. The mother loses her composure. She waves her arms in front of her as if trying to stop Policeman B. Policeman A is also surprised. He stands up and opens his mouth as if trying to say something, but words fail him, and he just mumbles something and stops. A minute of awkward silence passes.

Policeman B raises his voice to greet everyone present. He tries to maintain a normal, even tone.

POLICEMAN B

Hello, everyone. I am here only to find out more about what happened. Hi there, young man. Did you just get home?

The mother of the Amerasian, still surprised, remains silent. Policeman A regains his composure and calmly pulls a chair out to sit next to her.

POLICEMAN A

Please sit down and have some water. I just got here, too. I asked, and the young man said he had just returned from a business trip. So, is there anything that matters?

B doesn't stop observing the Amerasian. Under the light, his face looks tense, without a trace of cruelty. On the contrary, he looks naïve.

POLICEMAN B

(Mumbling)

Um... there are new facts...

(He changes his tone to sound very serious)

Well, since everybody is here now, I will give it to you straight. Folks from this hamlet have reported to the station that this Amerasian here has raped someone. My responsibility now is to investigate this rape. This afternoon I met with the victim. She has admitted to the relationship with this young man here. Young man, I have been looking for you the last few days, but couldn't find you. Now that I see you here, you must tell us the truth. You must tell us what you did. You cannot evade your responsibility and the law.

Policeman B stares at the Amerasian with a stern expression in his eyes as if he wants to hypnotize him.

Confused, the Amerasian looks the other way.

The mother regains her composure. She fires back in an irritated voice:

THE AMERASIAN'S MOTHER

As I told you the last time, my son has done nothing wrong. He's a good boy. He does honest work and doesn't do anything illegal. What right do you have to keep interrogating him? Don't go too far, or someone will sue you for illegally entering a home.

Policeman A follows up.

POLICEMAN A

My friend, don't be too quick to anger. Why are you bothering them? You have no proof; no one is denouncing them; what reasons do you have for pursuing them? Please don't push too hard as they might sue you for entering their home without a warrant.

Policeman B cannot contain his anger. He stands up.

POLICEMAN B

I understand you all too well. You, the Amerasian over there, you are a criminal, and I have proof. Follow me to the station, so that I can obtain your confession. And don't make any fuss.

Policeman B pulls out the handcuffs and then walks toward the Amerasian. Policeman A stands up and steps in front of Policeman B.

POLICEMAN A

How dare you do this while I am here? Where is your arrest warrant? He is at home, and he has not been caught in the act of committing a crime. You are a policeman. Don't you know the law?

The two policemen glare at each other. Policeman B screams:

POLICEMAN B

Are you protecting a criminal?

POLICEMAN A

(Snickering)

I am protecting the people and upholding the law.

POLICEMAN B

Protecting the people or protecting a criminal? How big

was the bribe you received to become so engaged?

POLICEMAN B

Protecting the people or protecting a criminal? How big was the bribe you received to become so engaged?

POLICEMAN B

You are the one who must get out, so that I can perform my duty.

Both policemen scream "get out!", and each grabs his gun, but neither pulls it out.

As the policemen argue, the Amerasian quietly slips out the back door and disappears into the night. Now only God can catch him.

From the corner of his eyes, B sees the Amerasian disappear as A's big frame blocks the view in front of him.

POLICEMAN B

Fine. I will think about it.

Policeman B says angrily and then walks out hurriedly.

53. THE STREET – OUTSIDE – MORNING

The man sits quietly outside behind a pile of books. Every once in a while, he opens one of these ancient and decrepit books and reads the table of contents or wipes the dust away from the cover.

Absorbed in his thoughts, he is startled when a truck stops noisily beside him, and the screams reach his ears. He still does not understand what is happening when several men jump out of the truck, grab the nylon sheet on which his books are displayed, and throw it, along with the books, onto the truck bed. Some of the books fall onto the street.

Several other men run out of their hiding places and rush to the stalls nearby. They upend everything and throw whatever they can grab onto the truck. They do so despite the protestations, pleadings, and screams of the owners.

All kinds of stuff is piled on the truck bed: furniture, books, glasses, bread, fruits, cigarettes, shoes, sandals, vegetables, and legumes. All mix together in a messy heap as the truck starts rolling.

The man stands motionless on the sidewalk. When he regains his wits, everything is eerily silent, as though a battle had taken place. He takes a good look around. They even took his wobbly stool. Ah, there is a book that escaped the raid and is lying on the ground! He bends down to pick it up. It is the Tale of Kiều.

He clutches the book to his chest and slowly walks away. Two verses from the Tale reverberate in his head:

If yours is a drifting fate, be resigned to it,

If yours is a noble fate, be content with it.

And the last wishes of the book's author, Nguyễn Du also come to mind:

No one knows if three hundred years hence

Someone will still cry for Tố Như

Tears suddenly start streaming down his cheeks. Tố Như, Kiều, I am crying for you two noble souls with such an unfortunate fate in this heart-wrenching life!

54. THE GRASSY HILL – OUTSIDE – NIGHT

The girl walks out of the house and heads toward the hills. She walks as if in a daze. Her shadow flickers on the desolate, grassy hills.

Night comes as she stumbles and makes her way to the end of a chain of hills. A large shadow rises from the side of the hill. The two recognize each other, show no surprise, and then embrace each other while tumbling onto the ground.

The Amerasian kisses the girl on the lips, and she clumsily returns the kiss. The two shadows merge into one on top of the soft grass and within the forgiving darkness. They keep kissing, taking in their waiting souls as their bodies are intimately wrapped around each other and writhing as if in a trance.

A long time afterward, they separate and lie on their backs looking up at the sky. Some stars are already shining in the darkening sky. Heaven and earth are quiet. Only the two of them exist and draw breath in this life.

THE GIRL

I wish we could be together forever like this. I wouldn't want anything else.

THE AMERASIAN

Me, too. But the sad thing is, we can't romanticize.

A policeman almost nabbed me last night. He even had handcuffs. Luckily I was able to run away. I really shouldn't be here with you tonight, but I missed you so much that I took the chance.

THE GIRL (sitting up now)

O, my God! It is so dangerous. What do we do now?

THE AMERASIAN

It's all my fault.

It is because of my black skin and the Amerasian blood coursing through my veins.

It is because I was not able to control myself and did what should not be done.

The girl presses her head against the Amerasian's chest. He strokes her hair. His hand is as black as her hair. The girl tries to comfort him.

THE GIRL

Please don't say that. Black skin isn't ugly, and you aren't guilty of anything.

Tiêu Dao Bảo Cự | 107

> Your skin may be black, but your heart is not.
>
> You did something wrong, but you have repented.
>
> If I forgive you, no one else can condemn you.

The Amerasian buries his hand deep into the flowing hair that covers his chest.

> **THE AMERASIAN**
>
> You understand and forgive me, but society doesn't.
>
> You and I are small and weak, while they are strong and have all the power.
>
> If that is not so, why would we be hiding and meeting in secret in this deserted place and at night?

The girl becomes distressed and angry at the bitter tone of his voice. She sits up and opens her eyes wide.

> **THE GIRL**
>
> I am not afraid of the dark night and the isolation.
>
> I don't even need a light. But I do need you, even though you are blacker than the night.
>
> Do you know that?

The Amerasian sits up, too, and grabs her shoulders tightly. She starts to sob. Her warm tears fall on his black hand even though he doesn't see them. He tries to console her.

> **THE AMERASIAN**
>
> Please try to stop crying. Let's not talk about it

> anymore, come what may. We should talk about happy things and not sad things when we meet. Look, the moon is up now.

The two of them look toward the east. On the faraway horizon, the tree line has turned dark black. The new and rising moon now casts a clear and magnificent yellow light that drives away the darkness of the night.

A light, golden glow covers the black mountains in front of the couple and makes them shimmer darkly, but not menacingly.

The two of them put their heads together to watch the moon rising slowly from the horizon. A golden light now bathes the surrounding area as a thin fog starts to spread its mystery around.

The girl becomes a little happier, and then even sadder. She looks at the black face of the Amerasian and sees that he has become shinier and less black in the golden moonlight.

THE GIRL

> The darkness of the night protects us, but it is the light that lets us see our true faces.
>
> Don't you want to see mine, too?

The Amerasian is startled by what she has said and turns his face to look at her. He sees how her hair, which shines as if flecked with gold, frames her face with the big, black, moist eyes and enticing pink lips. He suddenly bursts out.

THE AMERASIAN

Gosh! You are as pretty as a fairy, or as the angel painted on icons I have seen.

Why shouldn't I look at you? You shine a brighter light on my life than the moon up there.

You have brightened my life and my black skin.

We need light, but we also need darkness because we are being pursued. However, whether it is light or darkness, what matters is that we have each other; we are next to each other.

Isn't that so?

He bends down and kisses the young woman to stop her from saying aloud the sad and depressing thoughts that he knows are starting to invade her mind.

They sit and hold each other tightly. The moon rises higher and higher and spreads a golden yellow light over the earth. The shadows these two human beings cast on the empty grassy hill is just a tiny, black fleck on the immense earth and under the night sky.

55. THE GRASSY HILL - OUTSIDE - NIGHT

After a few ecstatic minutes and as the Amerasian and the girl stand up and prepare to leave, a black silhouette appears right in front of them. It is policeman B. The couple is totally taken aback. B raises his voice to speak.

POLICEMAN B

You the Amerasian. Where can you run to now?

The couple stand silent and speechless. Policeman B continues in a triumphant voice.

POLICEMAN B

You the Amerasian. Cat got your tongue, hey? Now can you still deny what you did? What are you doing here in the dark of the night trying to seduce an underage girl? Try to say something, will you? Now can I arrest you?

It takes a moment for the Amerasian to regain his wits. He wants to run away but because he is standing behind the girl, he hesitates. Suddenly, the girl pushes him to the side, steps up and stands between him and the policeman.

THE GIRL

You can't arrest him. He didn't do anything wrong.

POLICEMAN B

Aha! Are you trying to defend him? This is really getting out of hand! Hey you, the Amerasian, you are really good, you are a real professional seducer…

THE GIRL

Run!

She suddenly screams and lunges toward the chest of the policeman to push him away. Surprised by her prodigious attack, policeman B falls to the ground on his back. The

Amerasian darts away like an arrow and disappears in the dark night. Policeman B pushes himself up with his arms and stands back up. He stretches his arm out so as to slap the girl on her face but seeing that the Amerasian is gone, he exhales, relents and drops his arm.

He stands there and looks at the girl for an instant. His eyes glisten in the dark and hazy night. She stands firm like a strong young pine tree alone under the sky on a grassy and lonely hill. He walks away slowly.

56. THE STREET – OUTSIDE – MORNING

The father of the girl overcomes his dizziness and picks up the Tale of Kiều. He clutches it to his chest and spends the entire day wandering the streets like a madman.

57. THE SIDEWALK – OUTSIDE – AFTERNOON – DARK

In the afternoon the man goes into a bar, orders a liter of distilled rice wine, and drinks it slowly until night falls.

He sits alone at a dirty table. The odor of food, beer, and wine hangs heavily in the air. He pays no attention to the noises around him.

He just sits there slowly sipping his wine. He refills his cup as soon as he empties it and drinks until the last drop of wine is gone.

A large, middle-aged man, who is sitting at a nearby

table drinking with his friends, observes the man discreetly from afar. This middle-aged man is Policeman A in street clothes. He stands up, walks toward the man sitting alone, pulls out a chair, and then sits down while asking absent-mindedly:

POLICEMAN A

You look so sad! Why ?

The man looks up, perplexed but doesn't respond. He doesn't understand why someone is talking to him and what he is being asked. Policeman A smiles and repeats his question.

POLICEMAN A

Why do you look so sad? Drinking to drown your sorrows?

THE MAN

I drink when I am sad. But drinking doesn't release me from the sadness.

If anything, drinking intensifies the sorrow and the hatred.

POLICEMAN A

Why so much hatred for life?

THE MAN

Hatred for life…That's right…Hatred for life….

And how can it be otherwise? Do you have a child? If your child were raped, would you hate life? What would you do if people didn't allow you to work?

If given no alternative, if you were pushed into a corner, if your wife and kids are starving and suffering, wouldn't you be angry and hateful? You have a degree, right? If people trampled on your degree and treated it like a paper rag, wouldn't you be angry and hateful?

Huh? Huh? Tell me. Answer my question.

He mumbles and then lets the words pour out louder and louder, until he is screaming in the face of his interlocutor. The policeman shows no surprise; he simply takes a step back and looks at the man with his small, quizzical eyes. He nods his head.

POLICEMAN A

Indeed. One should hate. But if life is difficult, one must fight back and refuse to accept defeat.

THE MAN

(arching his eyebrows in surprise)

Fight back? I haven't heard those words in a long time

But how, and for what? Fight back against the government and go to jail or what? Even a tiny department head can lay you off if you displease him. As for denouncing the rapist who raped my daughter, do you really think I want everyone to know about it, especially given the fact that the rapist is an Amerasian?

What can a person like me do? What can I really do?

The man says these painful things to this perfect stranger, things he shouldn't say. But this stranger is far from uninterested. He wants to get the man to talk more.

POLICEMAN A

Regarding the rape of your daughter, especially by an Amerasian, for whatever it's worth, you really should denounce him in order to be compensated and to punish him.

THE MAN

It is impossible. My daughter doesn't want to denounce him, and, believe it or not, she even loves him.

He is being sponsored to go to America.

No one knows what will happen.

Everything... everything is so complicated. Anyhow, let it be... this life is so wretched... This is how things are.

The man's voice becomes slurred; his eyes glaze over; and his head slowly drops on the table. The policeman in plain clothes shrugs his shoulders and gets up. He turns toward his companions, who are sitting half drunk at a nearby table, picks up a bottle of beer, and starts to fill their glasses. He then raises his glass and loudly announces:

POLICEMAN A

Guys. Drink up! Bottoms up!

THE DRINKING BUDDIES

Go, Go, Go…

The "Go, Go, Go" screams resonate and mask the snoring sounds made by the small man hunched over the nearby table. A stream of tears has run down from the corner of his eye and blended in with the filth on the table.

57. THE INTER-VILLAGE ROAD – OUTSIDE –MORNING

Policeman B gets the news that a friend of his, a policeman in the next hamlet, has seen the Amerasian there. He im-mediately jumps on his motorcycle to go look for the Amerasian. He asks some villagers where the Amerasian has taken temporary refuge and then goes to find the place. It is a house at the end of the hamlet, next to the endless rows of tea bushes from a nearby plantation.

He walks into the courtyard of the house and is about to open his mouth to ask where to find him, when the Amer-asian happens to step outside. Seeing the policeman, the Amerasian panics and in a flash dashes toward the tea plan-tation. The policeman immediately starts running after him.

59. THE TEA HILL – OUTSIDE – MORNING

A deadly foot race between the two men ensues. The Am-erasian runs swiftly along the narrow path between two rows of tea trees, bending low to avoid tree branches and jumping over low bushes. Policeman B runs almost right behind him.

The distance between the two men lengthens over time. Policeman B pulls out his gun and shoots into the air. Startled, the Amerasian turns his head and stumbles on a large tree root. He falls to the ground, and the pain is so intense that he cannot get up immediately. Policeman B manages to catch up to the Amerasian, but then falls down next to him. The two of them look at each other, both breathing heavily and unable to say anything.

Once he recovers from the exertion, Policeman B exhales with pleasure as he looks at the Amerasian beside him. He observes him intensely. The Amerasian is still lying flat on the ground, one leg stretched out, the other pulled up as if he were getting ready to sprint away again. His eyes are open so wide that it looks as if they may pop out. His long eyelashes don't move, and his fear is palpable. Policeman B taps the gun in his hand.

> POLICEMAN B
>
> You can't run away now! There is nothing to be afraid of.
>
> Let's talk calmly. You need to tell me everything.

The Amerasian attempts to sit up. Gradually he regains his wits.

> THE AMERASIAN
>
> I am not afraid. You have no right to arrest me.
>
> I didn't do anything wrong.

POLICEMAN B

Come on! Don't give me that crap. You know what I want. I am a policeman.

I can shoot you dead right here and now and then claim that you have committed some crime.

As you know, dead men don't talk.

I am a policeman, after all.

The Amerasian understands that what the policeman is saying is perfectly true. He thinks for a moment and then decides to tell the truth.

THE AMERASIAN

It is true that I did something that is not right with the girl. But I never forced her.

I love her, and she loves me.

She has forgiven me, and we will get married when she gets older.

Just normal stuff. Nothing illegal.

POLICEMAN B

(Raising his voice)

It is not that easy as you say. If raping a 16 years old girl is not coercion, then what is? Is this how you love? And what does she know about love? What you did is to seduce and use her. You want to marry her when she grows up? When will that be? You are going to America. What stops you from leaving and never coming back for her? No, you have everything to gain. You get to love, you get to rape, you get to go to America, and you don't have to pay for any of these things. The American blood cursing in your veins does make you different. Do you really think the all of us Vietnamese are stupid? With her here, don't you dare think that way. I punished Big Americans like your old man, so I can do a lot worse against a puny Amerasian like you.

The policeman speaks in an icy and cutting voice. But something stirs within the Amerasian. He sits up straight and looks the policeman straight in the eyes.

THE AMERASIAN

You are such a big man, and yet you understand nothing about love. My girlfriend and I have the right to love each other, regardless of race and age. We will just love each other and live together despite all the obstacles. I can, but do not have to, go to America. If I go, it will be for our future, so that we will be less miserable. I have two bloodlines. My country is both America and Vietnam. Unlike you, I harbor no hate in my heart. All I want is to love and be loved. All I want is to work and to live happily ever after. Is that a crime? Did I do anything wrong? Why do you hate me so much?

The Amerasian speaks with conviction. His eyes are glowing. The policeman raises his eyebrows to look at him. It is true that there is love between him and the girl. The policeman remembers what he saw the other day: two people holding each other tightly and walking toward the sunset, a loving couple. However, the policeman has some doubts as to the Amerasian's claims that he will return from Amer-ica. He lowers his voice and speaks menacingly.

POLICEMAN B

Do you swear you will come back for her? Who can guarantee that?

THE AMERASIAN

No one can guarantee that for me. But I swear I will return unless I die. I don't know if anyone believes me. But I know she believes me and will wait for me. We promised each other already.

POLICEMAN B

So you say you won't betray her. But what happens if you die before that? Won't she be on the losing end when that happens even if she loves you very much?

THE AMERASIAN

I will not die. I will come back for her. I will come back to marry her.

The Amerasian speaks with deep conviction and with all his heart. The policeman is moved hearing him speak and sits still without saying anything.

60. THE TEA HILL - OUTSIDE - MORNING

Suddenly the Amerasian pushes Policeman B hands away hard so that the gun drops to the ground. B lunges forward trying to catch the gun but the Amerasian is able to grab it first being closer to it. He lifts the guns, takes one step back, and aims the gun toward the policeman. B stops in his track and stares at the Amerasian.

THE AMERASIAN

Stand still, or I will shoot.

POLICEMAN B

Do you dare? Remember, I am a policeman. You will go to jail for life for shooting a policeman . Do you dare?

THE AMERASIAN

Take on step forward and I will shoot. I am not afraid. I am just defending myself.

The policeman considers the determination on the Amerasian's face and feels a little afraid. But he regains his poise and swifty changes the conversation.

POLICEMAN B

I know you won't dare shoot me. You aren't stupid enough to add more calamities to your fate when you still have a big unresolved problem. Let me ask you again: do you really love the girl?

POLICEMAN B

But you are an Amerasian and she is an under age girl.

THE AMERASIAN

The girl told me herself that love doesn't differentiate and accepts no boundaries. She is still young and she understands that. Why can't you?

As the Amerasian speaks passionately, policeman B lunges forward trying to grab the gun, however, the Amerasian quickly steps back to avoid him.

THE AMERASIAN

Stop or I will shoot. I mean it. I kill you, and then I will kill myself. Because if I let you catch me, for me it would be like death even if I am still alive. I will do what I say.

POLICEMAN B

Don't do that. Things being what they are, there is still a way out. Just give me back the gun and we will find a solution. I think my sympathy is with you.

THE AMERASIAN

Then why don't you drop this matter.

POLICEMAN B

I am thinking about it. But you know I do have responsibilities. Give me back my gun and then let sit down and talk. You don't know how to use the gun, it is very dangerous.

As he speaks, Policeman B waves his arms and in a surprise move slaps hard on the arm of the Amerasian thus making him drop the gun. Both men then take a crouching stance as if they are going to jump on each other at any moment. However, no one is willing to make the first move and so they stand there crouching and staring intensely at the other.

61. THE TEA HILL – OUTSIDE – MORNING

In a surprise move, the Amerasian steps sideways and then speeds forward like an arrow. The policeman rushes to pick up the gun, lifts it up and aims it at the Amerasian who is running away, his finger firmly on the trigger. The distance between him and the Amerasian is close enough that the policeman feels that with his sharp shooting skills, he can hit him in one shot.

He pulls hard on the trigger. But at the last second before the hammer strikes the bullet, he jerks the gun skyward. Once more, the Amerasian disappears right in front of him, and this time in full daylight and not in the dark night.

He stands up and looks at the green and sun-splashed tea hill that spreads around him. He picks a green tea bud, puts it in his mouth, and chews it. The tea leaves taste sweet rather than bitter and this lifts his heart, as if the bitter taste of defeat that he felt the last time is gone.

62. THE GRASSY HILL – OUTSIDE – AFTERNOON

It is only mid-afternoon when the girl leaves the house. After looking carefully around to make sure she is not being followed, the girl crosses the grassy hill and walks toward the mountain. She is going to meet the Amerasian because he is leaving tomorrow. She absolutely believes that he will come back after his trip.

The sky is gray. When she reaches the end of the grassy hill, a light rain begins to fall and then grows heavier. She feels nervous as she looks at the darkening sky. The air quickly turns cold. The rain drenches her clothes, whips her face, and streams down her cheeks and lips. She runs erratically toward the mountain at the bottom of the hill. "Where are you? Where are you? How come you aren't here to meet me? If I lose you this afternoon, maybe I will lose you forever. Where are you? Where are you?" She calls out and raises her arms as if trying to protect her eyes from the stinging rain. She stumbles, falls, and then gets up to continue walking.

As the girl staggers and is beginning to feel desperate, out of the dark rain, the Amerasian appears. He, too, is totally drenched from head to foot by the rain. He grabs the girl, holds her tightly against his body, and runs very fast toward the bottom of the mountain.

63. THE MOUNTAIN GROTTO – INSIDE – AFTERNOON

The Amerasian takes her to a small and secluded grotto

that he found days ago while loitering around waiting for her. He picks a dry spot in the grotto that the rain cannot reach, sweeps it clean, and then spreads some dry grass and leaves over it.

The girl closes her eyes. She is shivering from the cold and the scratches she sustained when falling during her run on the hillside. The Amerasian is in a panic because both of them are soaking wet, and he doesn't know what to do. Overcoming his panic, he hurriedly removes his shirt, squeezes out the water, and then uses it to dry her face and hair. She is still shaking from the cold and her wet clothes. He hesitates for a moment and then speaks.

THE AMERASIAN

May I remove your clothes to better dry you off?

The girl nods weakly. He removes her clothes, squeezes out all the water, gently dries her off, and then uses his hands to rub her in order to warm her up. As he rubs the girl, all he is thinking is to help her fight off the cold, but as her body warms up, the contact between his hands and her body stirs him. God, how soft and white her skin is! Her small, budding breasts turn pink as he rubs them gently with his large, black hands. She is a girl just past puberty, full of life, and lying in his arms almost naked. Trembling, he kisses her forehead, eyes, lips, neck, and shoulders.

They embrace for a long time without saying anything except for asking each other if they are still cold. What they need to say to each other has already been said. All they want now is to be close to each other, to listen to each other's breath and heartbeat and feel the touch of each other's skin.

Suddenly, the Amerasian says in a faltering voice:

> **THE AMERASIAN**
>
> Do...do you want me to...?

The girl nods softly.

> **THE AMERASIAN**
>
> Aren't you afraid?

The girl shakes her head gently.

> **THE AMERASIAN**
>
> What...what if you become pregnant?

> **THE GIRL**
>
> I will give birth to and raise the baby. When you are gone, I will be very lonely and miss you very much. The baby will be the image of you, your flesh and blood. The baby will always be by my side to comfort me, just as you are for your mother.

The Amerasian and the girl herself are surprised that she has said all of this. The Amerasian is so happy he cannot speak. He falters.

> **THE AMERASIAN**
>
> Aren't you concerned that you will be unhappy...and poor?

THE GIRL

No. Because I love you, I can do anything.

The girl buries her head in the broad, strong chest of the Amerasian. He slowly lowers himself to the ground and pulls her down with him. He kisses her lips passionately.

The rain continues unabated outside. The wind howls over the treetops. Inside the grotto, the two lovers share everything: their bodies, their blood, and their souls. They grasp each other and writhe around as if trying to stay afloat as their passion carries them far away. They do not need or care for anything else. All worries, difficulties, and calcu-lations are swept aside. The small, unadorned grotto has become a heavenly sanctuary. Within it, black skin and white skin, innocence and lust, love and pleasure, taking and giving all blend together to create a mysteriously powerful brew that sets the lovers aflame. The fire of their love brightens the grotto, the sky, and the earth as the rainstorm continues to howl unabated outside.

FIVE YEARS LATER

64. THE GIRL'S HOME – INSIDE – AFTERNOON

A small, simple wedding is taking place at a house at the end of the isolated cemetery. The wedding has attracted the attention and gossip of many people in the town.

The groom is a young, tall Amerasian, He has curly hair, big bright eyes, and long, gentle eyebrows. He wears a white suit, a white shirt, and a red tie that together highlight the blackness of his skin as seen on his hands and face.

The bride is a young woman in her twenties. She looks mature and is extremely attractive. She wears little make-up, but her long, silky black hair, sparkling black eyes, and pink, sensuous lips give her oval face a lovely beauty that cannot be surpassed.

A little black-Asian boy, around four or five years old and wearing navy blue clothes and a pair of white sneakers is prancing around playfully. He asks for something, and all three of them break into laughter.

It is a belated wedding, held to honor a commitment made five years ago. Attending the wedding are the family of the bride, the mother of the groom, some adult friends of both families and, especially, the two policemen, whom the groom long ago suggested that the two families invite.

65. THE CEMETERY – OUTSIDE – AFTERNOON

After the ceremony to honor the ancestors, the acceptance of best wishes, and the reception luncheon and festivities, the bride and groom ask for permission to go outside for a while with their young son. They take the boy to the cemetery, burn incense at the large tomb and other tombs nearby, and then sit down at the same spot where they used to sit.

The young woman picks a tiny yellow flower growing near a crag and gives it to the man.

> THE WOMAN
>
> You know, this is the flower that was in bloom when we used to come here to talk.
>
> It kept blooming even after you left.
>
> Once the flower fades, it becomes a tiny clump to which very fine filaments are attached.
>
> These filaments then separate from the clump and fly away with the wind. I am this flower. I call these flowers the flying flowers.

The man picks up the flower, kisses it, and then puts it in the young woman's hair.

> THE MAN (THE AMERASIAN OF MANY YEARS AGO)
>
> I know. Over there, every now and then I used to catch one of these flying silk threads.
>
> It came from here, and I knew that you were still waiting for me.

And even this tiny flower that I pinned in your hair, too?

The man spreads his arms and embraces the mother and her child. All three smile. They are happy.

66. A GRASSY HILL – OUTSIDE – AFTERNOON

They sit together for a while and then walk toward the back of the house and in the direction of the grassy hill. The grassy hill hasn't changed: it remains desolate and lonesome in the afternoon sun and yet still so dear to them. The man lifts the boy up, points to the foothill, and speaks to the woman.

> THE MAN
>
> Do you remember the grotto over there?
>
> It was where we had our first wedding night five years ago.
>
> We truly belonged to each other and were forever linked from that moment.
>
> That small, dark grotto was our paradise and our private holy land.
>
> During my time in America, I always vividly remembered that grotto and the time we spent together there. It was as if I were there and alive. Do you want to go visit the grotto again with me, tomorrow? Do you agree?

The boy tugs at his father's hand.

> THE BOY
>
> I want to go there tomorrow, too. Please let me come with you.

The mother pinches her son's cheek.

> THE WOMAN
>
> Of course. Your life on this earth began there. Haven't I told you so many times before?

The boy claps his hands.

> THE BOY
>
> Yes, you told me. I was born there.

The young man pulls the woman closer to him. He speaks with emotion.

> THE MAN
>
> Not only were you born there, but all three of us were born there, too.
>
> There was only love, not hate, in that place. From there we three overcame everything to have what we have today.

The three of them look silently toward the mountain range. Their shadows dance on the grass under the endless afternoon sky.

CONCLUSION

67. – AT THE GIRL'S HOUSE - INSIDE - IN THE AFTERNOON

The emaciated old man rests his head on the table for a long time and then raises it slowly. He is old. His hair and beard have turned completely white. Like a dream, the happy scenario just described plays and replays in his head everyday, so that he almost believes it is true.

In reality, his daughter is sitting across from him. She is no longer the pretty little girl of many years ago. She has turned into an old woman. Her hair is disheveled; her clothes are dirty and wrinkled; and her eyes are lifeless.

Each afternoon, as the sun goes down, father and daughter sit together looking at the faraway mountain range and then turn their heads to look at the cemetery behind them. He dreams, but doesn't know what she is dreaming because she has gone mad. She just sits with empty eyes looking into the void and mumbling nonsense.

Sometimes he wonders who suffers more, he or his daughter. Neither the mountain range nor the cemetery on the horizon can deliver them from their misery. Can it be that when life is full of hatred and lies, the loss of one's mind is a blessing?

But suddenly, they hear noises coming from the gate. The old man and his daughter look up in surprise, their eyes wide open and mouths agape.

It is the Amerasian. He has returned. He is even taller than before. He is wearing a white suit with a red tie and lifting his arms as he rushes toward the house.

Dream or reality? Reality or dream? No one knows which is which. The rays of the setting sun light up the tombs in the darkening cemetery.

Author:
Tiêu Dao Bảo Cự
tieudaobaocu@gmail.com

Publisher
Nhân Ảnh
han.le3359@gmail.com
(408) 722-5626

www.ingramcontent.com/pod-product-compliance
Lightning Source LLC
Chambersburg PA
CBHW071856070526
44583CB00016B/1713